Studies in Economic Transition

General Editors: **Jens Hölscher**, Senior Lecturer in Economics, University of Brighton; and **Horst Tomann**, Professor of Economics, Free University Berlin

This new series has been established in response to a growing demand for a greater understanding of the transformation of economic systems. It brings together theoretical and empirical studies on economic transition and economic development. The post-communist transition from planned to market economies is one of the main areas of applied theory because in this field the most dramatic examples of change and economic dynamics can be found. The series aims to contribute to the understanding of specific major economic changes as well as to advance the theory of economic development. The implications of economic policy will be a major point of focus.

Titles include:

Studies in Economic Transition
Series Standing Order ISBN 0–333–73353–3
(*outside North America only*)

You can receive future titles in this series as they are published by placing a standing order.
Please contact your bookseller or, in case of difficulty, write to us at the address below with
your name and address, the title of the series and the ISBN quoted above.

Customer Services Department, Macmillan Distribution Ltd, Houndmills, Basingstoke,
Hampshire RG21 6XS, England

Financial Turbulence and Capital Markets in Transition Countries

Edited by

Jens Hölscher
Senior Lecturer
University of Brighton

First published in Great Britain 2000 by
MACMILLAN PRESS LTD
Houndmills, Basingstoke, Hampshire RG21 6XS and London
Companies and representatives throughout the world

A catalogue record for this book is available from the British Library.

ISBN 0–333–80041–9

First published in the United States of America 2000 by
ST. MARTIN'S PRESS, LLC,
Scholarly and Reference Division,
175 Fifth Avenue, New York, N.Y. 10010

ISBN 0–312–23531–3

Library of Congress Cataloging-in-Publication Data
Financial turbulence and capital markets in transition countries / edited by Jens Hölscher.
    p. cm. — (Studies in economic transition)
    Includes bibliographical references and index.
    ISBN 0–312–23531–3
    1. Capital market—Europe, Eastern. 2. Financial crises—Europe, Eastern. 3. Europe, Eastern—Economic conditions—1989– I. Hölscher, Jens. II. Series.

    HG5430.7.A3 F56 2000
    332'.0947—dc21

                                      00–034517

This book is printed on paper suitable for recycling and made from fully managed and sustained forest sources.

10   9   8   7   6   5   4   3   2   1
09 08 07 06 05 04 03 02 01 00

Printed and bound in Great Britain by
Antony Rowe Ltd, Chippenham, Wiltshire

Contents

List of Tables

List of Figures

Acknowledgements

This book is based on papers and discussions held at a conference at Klaffenbach-Water-Castle in February 1999. Generous financial support of the Commerzbank-Foundation is gratefully acknowledged. Colleagues of my faculty at Chemnitz University enthusiastically supported this event and I enjoyed far-reaching collaboration during my academic year as visiting professor to the Commerzbank-Chair for Money and Finance. Particular thanks go to Jens Dietrich and Daniel Nobis, who assisted me in convening the conference and Ralph Enzmann, who worked as an excellent editorial assistant of this book.

Kleinmachnow
Jens Hölscher

Notes on the Contributors

Harald Battermann is Economics Lecturer at the University of Paderborn after he served as Lecturer at Chemnitz University. His publications concentrate on risk and uncertainty.

Claudia Buch is Research Fellow at the Kiel Institute for the World Economy and Head of the Research Group 'Financial Markets'. She has published extensively in the field of the economics of transition.

Udo Broll is Visiting Professor at the University of the Saarland after he held Visiting Professorships at various other German Universities including Bonn and Munich. His publications concentrate on international trade and hedging.

Stephen F. Frowen is Fellow of St. Edmund's College, University of Cambridge, and a Senior Research Associate at the College's Von Hügel Institute, an Honorary Research Fellow in the Department of Economics at University College London, and Honorary Professor of the Institute of German Studies, University of Birmingham. Prior to these appointments he was Bundesbank Professor of Monetary Economics in the Free University of Berlin. For many years he held senior teaching posts at the Universities of Surrey and Greenwich and was Research Officer at the National Institute of Economic and Social Research, London. Visiting Professorships included the Universities of Frankfurt and Würzburg. He has published widely on monetary economics and related subjects. He was awarded the Grand Cross of the Order of Merit of the Federal Republic of Germany in 1993 and a Papal Knighthood in 1996.

Stephan Herten is Economics Lecturer at the University of Leeds Business School and PhD candidate at the Institute for German Studies of the University of Birmingham. He studied at the Universities of Heidelberg, Bonn and Berlin (FU), where he subsequently took up an appointment as Research Fellow. He has published in the areas of transition economics, input-output analysis and federalism.

Jens Hölscher is Senior Lecturer at the University of Brighton. Previously he served as Senior Fellow at the University of Birmingham and as

Lecturer at the University of Wales Swansea and Berlin Free University. He held Visiting Professorships at the Halle Institute for Economic Research, Chemnitz University and the Kazakhstan Institute for Management, Economics and Strategic Research. Publications concentrate on monetary and transition economics.

Alexander Karmann is Professor in Economics, especially Monetary Economics, at the University of Technology Dresden, since 1993. After a diploma in Mathematics, he was assistent and Privatdozent, until 1986, at the University of Karlsruhe where he passed his first and second PhD ('Habilitation') in Economics and Statistics. From 1986–1993 he was Professor in Economics at the University of Hamburg. He has published in the fields of Regional Economics, Monetary and Financial Economics.

Thomas Linne is Research Fellow within the Eastern Europe Department of the Halle Institute for Economic Research. His publications concentrate on transition economics.

Roman Matousek is Research Fellow at the Czech National Bank. He has published in the areas of monetary and transition economics.

Zbigniew Polanski is Professor at the Warsaw School of Economics (Chair of Monetary Policy) and Adviser to the Governor at the National Bank of Poland (Research Department). He obtained his PhD in Economics and Finance at the Warsaw School of Economics. In the early 1990s Dr Polanski was affiliated with the University of Maryland, USA, and the Carleton University in Ottawa, Canada. He has published many papers and several books on money and banking during the post-communist transformation.

Bruno Schönfelder, Professor of Economics at the Freiberg University of Mining and Technology (Bergakademie Freiberg), Faculty of Business Administration and Economics. Born in 1956, he was educated at the University of Munich and the University of Minnesota, Minneapolis. Both his Dr rer pol and his Dr rer pol habil are from the University of Munich. After teaching at the University of Rostock and serving as an adviser to the National Bank of Croatia he joined Freiberg University in 1992. His current research focuses on post-communist economies, in particular Croatia, the Czech Republic, Serbia and the Slovak Republic. He has published on a broad range of topics from theoretical as well as applied economics.

Vladislav I. Semenkov is Associate Professor at the Academy of Labour and Social Relations, Moscow, Russia. He secured his PhD from the Institute of World Economy and International Relations in Moscow. His main fields of interest are economies in transition and comparative economic systems. In 70s he was worked in the UNESCO, Paris. In 1995–1997 he has taught as a visiting lecturer at the University College London. He has published several books and articles on economic development, technological change and economics of transition.

Johannes Stephan is Research Fellow within the the Eastern Europe Department of the Halle Institute for Economic Research. After studies in Berlin, Munich and London he took his PhD at Birmingham University. His publications concentrate on the economics of transition.

Anita Taci is Research Fellow at the Institute of Economics, Czech Academy of Sciences and has published in the area of financial markets in transition economics.

Adam Török is President of the National Committee for Technological Development in Hungary after he served as Director of the Research Institute of Industrial Economics of the Hungarian Academy of Sciences and Professor at Budapest University of Technology and Economics and Central European University. He published extensively in the areas of technological development and transition economics.

Horst Tomann, born in 1940, is Jean Monnet Professor for European Economic Policy at the Economics Department, Freie University of Berlin. He received his academic education at the Universities of Cologne and the Saarland and was a staff member at the German Council of Economic Experts. His main research field is applied economics with a special focus on the economics of European integration. Research cooperation with the European Union Center, University of Pittsburgh and CERGE, Charles University of Prague.

František Turnovec is Professor of Economics at the Charles University, Prague, Center for Economic Research and Graduate Education (CERGE), from 1994–1999 Director of CERGE, and senior researcher at the Economics Institute of the Academy of Sciences of the Czech Republic. He is teaching public choice, microeconomics and European integration courses at Charles University and previously taught at the Institute for Advanced Studies, Vienna, Academia Istropolitana Nova, Bratislava,

Economics University, Bratislava and Agricultural University, Nitra. Author of articles on public choice, public economics, game theory and operations research. From 1992–1998 he was Co-editor of Central European Journal for Operation Research and Economics, currently he is a member of editorial boards of several professional journals.

Uwe Vollmer is Professor of Economics at the University of Leipzig. Born in 1958 he studied economics at Ruhr-Universität Bochum. In 1987 he had the opportunity to do research at the International University of Japan, Tokyo. He is a member of the 'Ausschuss für Wirtschaftssysteme' of the 'Verein für Socialpolitik' (German Economic Association) and of the 'Forschungsseminar Radein zum Vergleich von Wirtschafts-und Gesellschaftssystemen, e.V.'

Adalbert Winkler studied economics at the University of Trier and at Clark University, Worcester, Mass. He received his doctorate in 1992 while serving as a research assistant in the Department of Money, Credit and Finance at the University of Trier. Since 1994 he has headed the economic research department at Internationale Projekt Consult (IPC), a consulting company which specializes in development finance and carries out financial institution building projects worldwide. Dr Winkler also serves as a lecturer at the University of Würzburg. His main fields of research are monetary and financial economics and the economics of transition.

Introduction

This work provides an assessment of consequences of global financial turbulences on capital markets in transition countries. A sample of four countries shows the divergence of the emergence of capital markets during transition from planned to market economies.

'The Return of the Habsburgs' is the title of Horst Tomann's keynote address. Tomann thereby sets the agenda for the general topic. Four countries in transition from planned economies towards market economies are under review: Russia, Poland, the Czech Republic and Hungary. He points out that the theme of the conference signals that capital markets do exist in the transition countries, where financial substitutes are traded and financial intermediation is deepening and that these capital markets are sufficiently open to become vulnerable to global turbulences. Tomann further emphasizes the importance of financial institutions in establishing a system of viable property rights, although the financial sector in particular needs elements of spontaneous order in the Hayekian sense. There are good reasons for regulating financial markets to avoid the externalization of market risks by leverage trading, adverse selection, moral hazard and so on. On the other hand, the spontaneous order of liability, trust and stable expectations cannot evolve, if the government controls the financial markets for its own ends. The experience of the last ten years has shown, how a deregulation of underdeveloped financial markets can boost economic developement, if it is complemented by *Ordnungspolitik* as a response to uncertainty.

The second general chapter by Herten and Hölscher asks whether transition economies should follow the 'Anglo-Saxon' or 'Rhenish' model of capital market organization. The authors argue in favour of the German type of a universal bank based system in order to write off bad assets of the past. In their view such an orientation requires a strategy of 'semi-liberalization'.

The country studies of this book open with a report about Russia, the 'eye of the hurricane', by Vladislav Semenkov. He examines the question, who (or what) is really to be blamed not only for the recent financial crisis but for the general disorientation of the Russian reforms which paved the way for the crisis of 1997–98. There seem to be many explanations available, beginning with the irresponsible policy of the

Central Bank of Russia to the delayed devaluation of the rouble. Semenkov argues that, in contrast to the previous crises, the currency crisis of 1997–98 was not unavoidable, although the debt crisis in the state financial sector was a direct consequence of the dramatic financial situation in the real sector. Tax increases introduced in 1997 turned out to be unrealistic for formerly successful enterprises. This led to a steady reduction of the state budget income and to the need to borrow in the external and internal securities markets with the result of a rapid growth in the domestic state debt. The increasing dependence of the Russian economy on external forces became evident in this development, especially Russia's attempts to attract non-resident's resources for state obligations. At the first signs of the Asian financial crisis these non-residentials withdrew their hot money for reinvestment in the safer US markets and initiated a cumulative capital-flight-inflation cycle.

Semenkov's second question concerns: 'What to do?' He concludes that perhaps the Russian markets needed the shock of a crisis in an attempt to get rid of its two main disproportions: the domination of foreign capital and the underdevelopment of their market infrastructure which discouraged investments in the real sector. Semenkov suggests an agenda based on a pilot project proposed by experts from the Council of Federations and economists from his Academy of Sciences which are based upon principles of the so-called 'mobilization model':

1 Mobilization of all non-fiscal sources of state budget income;
2 Centralization of currency resources of the country and de-dollarization of the banking system;
3 Strict control of price formation and operations in natural monopolies up to the re-nationalization of some of them;
4 Re-nationalization of some bankrupt enterprises;
5 Re-orientation of money and credit policies towards production, accompanied by adequate regulation of interest rates and money flows;
6 Radical suppression of organized crime and eradication of corruption of the state bureaucracy;
7 Protection of rights of private and public property, promotion of competition and anti-monopoly control in commerce;
8 Adoption of measures of protection of domestic markets; and
9 Promotion of active industrial, structural and technological policy.

The discussants of Semenkov's contribution, Thomas Linne and Adalbert Winkler contend, that despite Semenkov's explanations, it is not yet clear why this financial crisis was so severe. They decide this crisis was so severe because it was more a crisis in the international financial market rather than in the Russian financial market. Even though Russia was unable to sustain its stabilization policy due to the failure to limit budget deficits, and even though at the heart of the problem is the instability of the banking system, these conditions are not new phenomena in the Russian transition process and have occurred periodically since 1992. The very special problem of Russia during the international financial crisis in 1998 (the Asian crisis) was that it had no central bank which could serve the commercial banks as *lender of last resort*, because the majority of the withdrawn deposits was denominated in foreign currencies. Therefore the problem of the international financial crisis was one concerning Russian commercial banks, regardless of monitoring the quality of their credit portfolios. According to Winkler the only way to overcome the consequences of such international financial crises would be to establish an international lender of last resort.

The second country study in the context of financial turbulences considers Poland and starts with an analysis by Zbigniew Polański. He emphasizes that Poland is one of the few transition countries that has not visibly suffered from the worldwide financial turbulences of the second half of the 1990s. Thus, the question emerges: Why has Poland, contrary to its close neighbours, been immune from these phenomena? Is Poland immune to contagion? Polański offers some explanations to this question: The Polish economic policy of the 1990s, which stresses a need for solid fundamentals, is the main reason behind the fact that Poland proved to be immune to 'financial contagion'. Macroeconomic stability was combined with a step-by-step approach of ongoing bank privatization and consolidation. Even the growing current account deficit seems to be sustainable due to the sound way of financing it.

The discussant of Polański's paper, Alexander Karmann, agrees that the Polish economy has continued its fast-pace growth at the time of the Asian-Russian crisis. A crucial role for defending Central European transition countries from the financial problems of Asia and Russia has been played by the close relationship with Germany and the programme of the EU to prepare Poland, the Czech Republic and Hungary for EU-membership.

The third study is dedicated to the Czech Republic and begins with the report of František Turnovec. He concentrates on the ownership structure of the Czech ecomony in general and in detail on the banking system to evaluate their impacts on the economic performance of the country. He compares the primary 'face' of the property structure to the real position of the subjects of property rights and records a significant difference between them. Empirical evidence indicates that the true value of the state's share in the Czech banking sector is significantly higher than it appears on the basis of primary property distribution. The general conclusion is that formally privatizing x per cent of former state property might still keep the state responsible for considerably more than $(100 - x$ per cent), taking into account indirect property distribution. Existing evidence indicates that the rapid Czech privatization was a rather complicated way of switching from inefficient, but more transparent public property to still not very efficient and at the same time less transparent public property. The illusion of privatization and the state's refusal to guarantee private property rights as well as the absence of a reasonable doctrine of temporary state capitalism contributed to the present problems of the Czech economy and Czech society.

The first comment on Turnovec by Claudia Buch asks in continuation to Turnovec: What is special about the Czech Republic? For Buch it is the failure to decisively reform institutions and corporate governance systems, which was hidden behind a curtain of macroeconomic success and now makes a recovery from the crisis in 1997 painful. She argues that the ownership pattern in the Czech financial market is a key factor behind financial market developements. Her analysis focuses on the crucial role of the banking sector in providing sound domestic governance structures and in enhancing financial stability. Banks' weak incentives have eventually contributed to the poor performance of the Czech economy, while the problems of the banking sector and the recent balance of payment crisis are merely two sides of the same coin. In contrast, the second comment by Bruno Schönfelder doubts that even such refined measurement of transparency of ownership would measure something of real economic significance. Transparency of ownership structures as defined by Turnovec and social welfare would presumably be unrelated. Yet, cross-ownership structures might be welfare-enhancing, especially in transition countries, because it provides protection against unfriendly take-overs. It also supports long-term relations and enables the involved parties to invest in relation-specific assets without running the risk of a hold-up. Furthermore it may enhance managerial independence which in turn may be particularly desirable if the ultimate owner happens to be the government. Last not least, Schönfelder tackles the issue of state co-owned companies and exemplifies this in respect to interlocking shareholderships in Germany, Austria, France, Sweden and Italy, maintaining that there is no necessity in such ownership structures for economic failure.

The part on the Czech Repaublic is completed by a chapter from Roman Matoušek and Anita Taci, who analyse the role of small and medium sized banks within the Czech financial sector.

The last country study examines the economic situation and prospects of Hungary beginning with an analysis by Ádám Török. He reviews Hungary's development from an underdeveloped financial market with heavily indebted state-owned banks and almost astronomical gross foreign debt to the best performing EU-candidate country of the Visegrad-group. The beginning of the reform of the financial sector was the spectacular and, in Hungary widely welcomed, re-establishment of a two-tier banking system. The dramatic deterioration of the quality of the portfolio of the commercial banks after this reform followed from a former strategic mistake committed by the government: the two-tier system was created on a state-owned basis, the lack of transparent criteria for lending then combined with *de facto* missing corporate governance which made granting credit to low-quality debtors a regular practice. The true condition and performance of the Hungarian banks became visible in 1992. As a result, most of them turned out to be unable to survive without government help. This bank consolidation process had to be completed with the privatization of all commercial banks in Hungary. But Török points out that the private ownership of commercial banks is no remedy against poor performance. Only the integration of most Hungarian banks into multinational networks of banking systems offers a strong guarantee of sound corporate governance. This time the decreased relative share of bad assets within the portfolio of the Hungarian banking sector marked the end of financial turbulences within the Hungarian economy.

Török's analysis of the Hungarian way through financial turbulences is discussed by Johannes Stephan and Uwe Vollmer. Stephan agrees with Török on almost every point and only accentuates some of the arguments raised in his analysis. He underlines the importance of the re-establishment of a two-tier banking system as a fulfilment of the paramount condition for the functioning of a monetary constitution in a modern monetary economy. Only divorce of the money supply from the commercial banking system can systemically introduce *derived scarcity* of money. Vollmer stresses the importance of increased competition within the banking sector.

Finally Stephen F. Frowen takes the reader through the broader context of the subject 'Financial markets in Eastern Europe'. The text, which was presented as pre-dinner speech, is reprinted here in its original style. Frowen points to the central issue, that is the importance of sound financial markets and banking systems for the health of a national economy. This would be particular relevant for the process of successful transition towards market economies and for appeals to the international financial institutions, including the IMF and World Bank, to rethink their role in contributing to financial stability. Stressing the farreaching consequences of the globalization of financial markets and the turbulences at least partly caused thereby, with their distinct impact on money and capital markets in transition countries, he expresses a warning to the latter not to rush into EMU membership and the strait jacket of the Maastricht Treaty. Instead, they would in his view be well advised to retain their sovereignty over economic decision-making for quite some time. Financial stability, closely related to political stability, is created at home and cannot be imported from abroad. He feels that ECB measures to combine strong economic discipline with the avoidance of deflation have still to show their results and the politics involved may not at this stage be the optimal ones for transition countries. Frowen's speech is reflected by a theoretical note of Battermann and Broll.

It is hoped that this work advances the understanding of financial turbulences and might help to fine-tune economic policy within transition countries.

Jens Hölscher
Kleinmachnow

I
Keynote Address

1
The Return of the Habsburgs – Reflections on the Role of Institutions in Transition Economies

Horst Tomann[1]

Introduction

The theme 'Financial turbulences and capital markets in transition countries' is a very timely one. I will refer to this theme which will occupy us all day tomorrow only insofar as it signals that capital markets do exist in transition countries where financial substitutes are traded, where financial intermediation is deepening and last but not least that capital markets are sufficiently open to become vulnerable to global turbulences. This is by no means self-evident. After all, the transition period is still shorter than one decade. Also, capital markets' constitutions differ substantially from country to country. So, I think the editor made a wise decision to give a country-by-country structure to the programme and to begin with Russia, the eye of the hurricane.

In my keynote address I would prefer to direct your interest to the background of these actual financial developments and problems of macroeconomic stabilization. I would like to present some basic reflections on the relationship between integration and economic development, and the vehicle to do this is integration (of CECs) into the EU. This will lead me to some conclusions on the role of financial institutions.

1   The economist's parable

Eastern enlargement of the EU, when it will occur in the not too distant future, will be an act of integrating unequal partners: The Visegrad countries' GDP is small compared to the EU's (about 4 to 5 per cent);

3

the level of real income is on average lower than in the EU's objective 1 regions; technological standards and productivity levels are poor; market institutions are not working properly; and so on. In November 1995, *The Economist* titled a survey of Central Europe with the provocative slogan 'The Return of the Habsburgs'. Obviously, the economic integration of unequal partners can only be conceived of as an act of subjection and expropriation.

Being economists, we do not take that slogan at its face value, but would take a more optimistic stance in favour of enlargement. First, we would expect benefits for both partners as a consequence of opening up markets. As is well known, those benefits can be deducted in models of classical trade theory as the welfare effects of regional specialization. Also, modern growth theory provides a basis for this kind of reasoning, as far as growth depends on the production of knowledge and knowledge is being made available by integration (Jacobsen, 1999). It is also well known, however, that those effects are long-term effects since they depend on the prevalence of competition and structural change. In the contemporary world, these factors develop their beneficial outcomes only in the long run. Moreover, modern trade theory provides for another scenario, namely that an early exposure of the newly emerging industries to the competitive pressures of world markets, where imperfect competition prevails, may result in an international specialization which leads to divergence rather than convergence of economic development. The recipe is simple: take into account that economic development takes place in markets governed by monopolistic competition, suppose an indivisible set of production capacities and external economies of regional agglomerations, then the historical accident helps you to conclude that Central Europe will become Europe's new periphery.

So, economic theory would leave us in an indetermined position at best. However, Central European countries have to consider the *status quo* as well. What is the alternative? From the very beginning, the EU provided only inadequate market access to their suppliers. In particular, the Europe Agreements explicitly provide for measures against dumping (Article 29) and against trade which would damage the economic base of a region (Article 30), and so does the EU Treaty (Article 115). These provisions work as deterrents against trade in goods for which we would assume comparative advantages of Central Europe, particularly due to the low level of wages. Under these conditions, Central Europe is left with the option of accepting a system of managed trade. Their call for EU membership has to be evaluated against this background.

The second source of an economist's optimism is explicitly stated by *The Economist* in its survey. It is a very specific argument. Looking back into European history, *The Economist* recognizes:

> Through Renaissance, Enlightenment and balance-of-power wars, Central Europeans have undergone the western experience. The administrative and education systems they have today are rooted in Habsburg tradition.

It is this 'Habsburg spirit', *The Economist* concludes, which gives a head-start to central European countries in joining the EU. Actually, they are re-joining the EU, returning to their origin of western civilization. This thesis finds a remarkable parallel in Huntington's (1996) theory 'The clash of civilizations'. After the collapse of communism, there are no more political, economic or ideological conflicts in the world. It is now culture and tradition which makes the difference and, as a consequence, which defines Europe's borderline. Incidentally, this thesis has been warmly welcomed by Russian politicians and social scientists. The reason seems evident. Since the integrating power of Marxism-Leninism was fading, the fashionable 'culturology' has provided a new identity for the former Soviet Union (Scherrer, 1998).

However, I shall not treat the danger of a new ideology in disguise in my talk but will consider the hard core of the Habsburg thesis. From an economist's point of view, the important question is what role is assigned to institutions in economic development? Let me provide some reflections on the role of institutions (property rights) in a market society and on the deficiencies in institution building in transition economies. This in turn will offer a link to the conference theme. To begin, I will go through some estimates on the prospective effects of EU enlargement to the East.

2   Simulation estimates on enlargement: Baldwin, Francois and Portes

Richard Baldwin, after having launched a 'too poor, too populous and too agricultural to join' verdict on CECs in 1994, offers a political correct CEPR study in 1997 in cooperation with Joseph Francois and Richard Portes. Applying a simulation technique in a general equilibrium world model, the authors calculate beneficial effects of enlargement for CECs, the EU and the rest of the world. In a conservative scenario, taking allocative effects and effects on the growth of the capital stock into account, an EU entry increases CECs' exports by 25 per cent and real income by 1.5 per cent. The estimates of a less conservative scenario are more exciting. Here the authors assume that an entry into the EU by providing CECs with the *acquis communautaire* will reduce the risk premium on investment and, as a consequence, will increase the effects on real income substantially. Although the quantitative effects are widely disputed, the message is clear. The important effects of an entry are caused by the change in institutions. Baldwin *et al.* (1997) summarize the channels through which investors' expectations are influenced:

> On the micro side, EU membership greatly constrains arbitrary trade and indirect tax policy changes. It also locks in well-defined property rights and codifies competition policy and state-aids policy. By securing convertibility, open capital markets and rights of establishment, membership assures investors that they can put in and take out money. Finally, EU membership guarantees that CEEC-produced products have unparalleled access to the EU15 markets (which account for almost 30% of world income). On the macro side, membership puts the CEECs on a path to eventual monetary union and thus provides a solid hedge against inflation spurts. These two aspects of membership are likely to have a related impact on investor confidence and are likely to be mutually reinforcing.

3   It's institutions, stupid

The role of institutions in economic development has been widely recognized in the literature. The late Olson, for example, provided empirical evidence in one of his last studies that institutions explain national growth differences which cannot be captured by the old nor by the new growth theory. 'Legal systems that enforce contracts and protect property rights,... political structures, constitutional provisions, and the extent of special-interest lobbies and cartels' have an important impact on the level and growth of national income (Olson, 1996, p. 6). This applies particularly to transition economies since transition is genuinely institution building. For example, there was no financial sector in central planning – since there were no financial risks. So, in transition to a market economy, a financial sector has to emerge. What does that mean? The institutions of a market economy, if they are to work properly, do require above all a clear cut definition of property rights.

All the reform countries of Central and Eastern Europe have redefined their property rights. We observe a fundamental shift from stake-holder values to share-holder values. But although the institutional foundations of a capitalist market society have been established, not least with a view to the warranted EU membership, property rights were incompletely defined.

> All countries have emphasized the creation of a set of laws attuned to capitalism: constitutional protections for private property, anti-trust statutes, commercial codes, bankruptcy laws, foreign investment guarantees, and so on...missing are the appropriately structured agencies, effective courts, the customary practice of enforcing private rights, the professionals, the scholarly and judicial opinion, and the web of ancillary institutions that give substance to written law (Murrell, 1996, pp. 33f).

Evidently, the elements of a 'civic culture' (Olson) can only partly be established by political decision-making and by enacting laws. To a large extent they are part of a spontaneous order in von Hayek's sense which emerges as a response to an increasing demand for such rights in the context of market interactions. Rapaczynski has pointed out as a fundamental flaw in economic theorizing the usual procedure to presuppose a given set of property rights as a framework for the market process to work. By contrast, he states, there is a set of intangible rights which cannot be established by the government's legislative and enforcement activities but which are in turn an outcome of market interactions (Rapaczynski, 1996, p. 692). So we are left with a real problem. On first sight, we should query whether extension of the EU *acquis* towards East would provide a substantial improvement to CECs.

Let us have some second thoughts. The interrelationship between the emergence of institutions and economic development could indeed turn out to be an intractable problem. If it is true that institutions of a market society evolve in the process of economic development and at the same time economic development requires existing institutions, where shall we start? I propose to clarify in more depth the role of institutions in a civic society in order to come to a better understanding of the shortcomings in the process of transition.

4   State of the art: The Old and the New Institutionalism

Essentially, *Ordnungspolitik* is a response to uncertainty. Interactions in markets yield uncertain outcomes, and it is the role of the economic order to reduce this uncertainty, in particular the uncertainty on how agents behave. This aspect is particularly underlined by Rutherford (1994, p. 81):

> Institutions provide a basis for action in a world that would otherwise be characterized by pervasive ignorance and uncertainty (Hayek, O'Driscoll and Rizzo); that institutions create a degree of standardization and predictability of behaviour (Mitchell, Heiner); that they solve recurrent coordination problems (Lewis), prisoners' dilemmas (Ullmann-Magalit, Schotter) and other similar types of problems.

Those definitions take a specific focus on the behaviour of market agents. And that in turn explains why the required order for markets to work efficiently evolves in a spontaneous way.

The Old Institutionalism provides an explanation that can be traced back to the writers of the Enlightenment. Indeed, it is David Hume who most clearly formulates the problem. In his *Treatise on Human Nature* (1951, p. 479) he asks a hypothetical question:

> I suppose a person to have lent me a sum of money, on condition that it be restor'd in a few days; and also suppose, that after the expiration of the term agreed on, he demands the sum: I ask, *What reason or motive have I to restore the money?*

Hume's model case formulates the central problem of a capitalist society: it is the uncertainty in contractual relationships between creditors and debtors. The key to the solution of this problem is self-interest. It is in my interest to give the money back since my own property rights can only be secure if I do not question the property rights of others. Albert Hirschman (1977), in his famous '*The Passions and the Interests*' has demonstrated that this idea is the inheritance of Enlightenment (referring to Montesquieu). Market agents have to learn to tame their passions and transform them into mutual interests. It is this transformation which lends the market society a civilizing feature.

Based on this paradigm, the Old Institutional Economics (in particular v. Hayek, Menger, v. Mises) has developed the concept of a spontaneous order and has defined the role of institutions in a market society. It is part of this concept that a society's economic order emerges from market interaction and cannot be established by decree. As a consequence, an economic order, as far as it is a spontaneous order, cannot be imitated. So, transition countries take a chance if they imitate and adapt western institutions. The implantation of western institutions can only be part of a learning process by which viable property rights are eventually established.

The New Institutionalism underlines this result, and assigns a specific role to the government. New Institutional Economics was developed as a response to a neoclassical approach of modelling imperfect information. Whereas the neoclassical approach treats uncertainty as risk with the consequence that insurance arrangements become possible, New Institutional Economics defines uncertainty again as a fundamental problem of market interaction, which cannot be resolved by probabilistic methods. Referring to a Keynesian tradition of research (see in particular Muchlinski, 1998), New Institutionalism assigns the role of stabilizing expectations to the institutions of a market society.

That role can be performed by conventions that emerge spontaneously in the market process and that are self-enforcing. But government also has a role to play in stabilizing expectations. It is clear from Hume's model case that this requires the government to tie its hands. By following the rules of the game, a government can gain credibility which is a precondition if government actions are to have stabilizing effects on expectations.

Transition countries' governments face a specific problem here. They have to provide guarantees for the newly emerging property rights (Engerer, 1997) by establishing the institutions of a market economy. However, the viability of these property rights depends to a large extent on the condition that economic and political reforms are continued and successfully completed. A government cannot credibly promise to fulfil this condition – the successful completion of transition. A substantial uncertainty is left for private agents. The problem is aggravated because the government is not only the referee but also a player in the field. Also, many politicians have already lost credibility.

It is at this point that entry into the EU yields its beneficial effects. The *acquis* provides for the required credibility of CECs' governments. The promise that the reform process will be completed will gain credibility.

5   Deficiencies in institution building

From an economist's point of view, CECs by transforming their systems of property rights, have established regulations that insufficiently enforce the principle of liability. The new system of property rights is imbalanced since economic risks have been largely left with the government (Tomann and Scholz, 1996). There is ample evidence for this deficiency, the major obstacles being the government's role in merging private and state enterprises, the presence of insider ownership and network property, non-enforcement of bankruptcy laws, credit-chains in the non-banking sectors, non-payment of salaries and tax debts on the side of state enterprises and so on (Engerer, 1997). That is complemented on the part of the financial sector by preferential credits provided by the central bank and business banks with the consequence of continued prolongation of bad assets and revolving recapitalization of state banks; by forced savings as for private households, and finally by keeping the central bank dependent on the government's discretion. Such a constellation was modelled by McKinnon and others as a case of financial repression (Schrooten, 1999).

6 The role of financial institutions

The role of financial institutions in establishing a system of viable property rights is simple: clear the balance sheets and provide for what Janos Kornai has called hard budget constraints. That function cannot be fulfilled properly in a state of financial repression. So, governments have to overcome their motives underlying such a strategy, namely, to enforce a fiscal drag on financial resources and, perhaps also, to continue a strategy of central planning in disguise.

The financial sector in particular needs a spontaneous order. It is true, spontaneity can be overdone as the crisis of so-called hedge funds in the US has demonstrated. So, there are good reasons to regulate financial markets to avoid the externalization of market risks by leverage trading, adverse selection, moral hazard and so on. On the other hand, there is evidence that a spontaneous order of liability and trust cannot evolve if the government controls the financial sector to its own ends. The literature on financial repression in less developed countries demonstrates that a deregulation of underdeveloped financial markets boosts economic development. On the one hand, deregulation allows for the development of financial instruments that provide for a deepening of financial intermediation (Shaw, 1973). On the other hand, McKinnon (1973) has shown that money assets and real investments increase complementarily if financial markets in less developed countries are liberalized and that this is simple evidence for improved conditions of internal enterprise finance.

To sum up, let me stress two points: 1. financial markets more than other markets require a spontaneous order, that is trust and liability to work properly; 2. It is the role of the government to tie its hands. A formal liberalization of financial markets does not help if there is no guarantee for creditors' property rights and if a culture of non-payment is tolerated by the government.

Both conditions have to be fulfilled to provide for viable property rights. To me, the viability of property rights seems to be more important for economic development than the real rate of interest. Although we have to recognize that the transition to viable property rights is accompanied by an increase in real interest rates, a strategy of reducing the real rate of interest by financial repression and/or by inflation is not a sound base for economic development. It is in such circumstances that the following judgement holds true: there is no small devaluation for transition countries. But the reason is not the abolition of capital controls. It is rather that governments are not credible in their effects to provide for economic stability and growth.

Note

1 I gratefully acknowledge valuable comments and suggestions by Elke Muchlinski, though what follows is my responsibility.

References

Baldwin, R. E., Francois, J. F. and Portes, R. (1997) The Costs and Benefits of Eastern Enlargement: The Impact on the EU and Central Europe, *Economic Policy*, 24, 125–70.

Bofinger, P. (1995) Optionen für die Währungsordnung einer Europäischen Union der Zwanzig, paper presented at the DIW Symposion *Vertiefung und Osterweiterung der Europäischen Union – Konflikt oder Kongruenz?*, Berlin, November.

Csaba, L. (1998) On the EU-Maturity of Central Europe: Perceived and Real Problems, in *Europäische Integration als ordnungspolitische Gestaltungsaufgabe*, Schriften des Vereins für Socialpolitik, N.F. Bd. 260. Berlin: Duncker & Humblot, pp. 225–46.

Engerer, H. (1997) Eigentum in der Transformation – Grenzen der Privatisierung in Mittel-und Osteuropa, Dissertation, Freie Universität Berlin.

Hirschmann, A. O. (1977) *The Passions and the Interests – Political Arguments for Capitalism before its Triumph*, Princeton: University Press.

Hume, D. [1739/40] (1951) *A Treatise on Human Nature*, Oxford: L. A. Selby-Bigge.

Huntington, S. (1996) *The Clash of Civilizations and the Remaking of World Order*, New York: Simon & Schuster.

Jacobsen, A. (1999) *Zentralosteuropäische Wachstumsperspektiven im Handel mit der Europäischen Gemeinschaft*, Aachen: Shaker.

McKinnon, R. (1973) *Money and Capital in Economic Development*, Washington DC: Brookings Institution.

Muchlinski, E. (1998) Konventionen im Rahmen der Institutionenökonomik – eine Kritik, in G. Wegner, and J. Wieland (eds), *Formelle und informelle Institutionen. Genese, Interaktion und Wandel*, Marburg, 279–308.

Murrell, P. (1996) How Far Has the Transition Progressed?, *Journal of Economic Perspectives*, 10, 2, 25–44.

Olson, M. (1996) Distinguished Lecture on Economics in Government: Big Bills Left on the Sidewalk: Why Some Nations are Rich, and Others Poor, *Journal of Economic Perspectives*, 10, 2, 3–24.

Rapaczynski, A. (1996) The Roles of the State and the Market in Establishing Property Rights, *Journal of Economic Perspectives*, 10, 2, 87–104.

Rutherford, M. (1994) *Institutions in Economics. The Old and the New Institutionalism*, 2nd edn, 1996, Cambridge: Cambridge University Press.

Scherrer, J. (1998) Kulturologie – ein neues Konzept für altes Denken? *Berliner Osteuropa Info*, 11/1998, Osteuropa-Institut der Freien Universität Berlin, 6–11.

Schrooten, M. (1999) Geld, Banken und Staat in Sozialismus und Transformation – vom Zusammenbruch der Sowjetunion zur anhaltenden Finanzkrise in der Russischen Föderation, Dissertation. Freie Universität Berlin.

Shaw, E. S. (1973) *Financial Deepening in Economic Development*, New York. Oxford University Press.

The Economist (1995) The Return of the Habsburgs. A Survey of Central Europe, 18, November.

Tomann, H. and Scholz, O. (1996) Strukturwandel und Soziale Sicherung, in J. Hölscher *et al.* (eds), *Bedingungen ökonomischer Entwicklung in Zentralosteuropa*, volume. 4, Elemente einer Entwicklungsstrategie, Marburg: Metropolis.

2
'Anglo-Saxon' or 'Rhenish' Financial Markets for Central-East Europe?

Stephan Herten and Jens Hölscher

1 Introduction

The question of this analysis is whether the transition countries in Central-East Europe should choose the Anglo-Saxon type of financial markets or the Rhenish bank-based system of financial sectors as orientation in building up new domestic capital markets and in the process of moving towards a mature market economy. The underlying assumption is that, like Schumpeter's (1911) banker as 'ephor of the exchange economy', a sound financial system is crucial for the functioning of economic systems, in particular for the process of development such as the transition from planned economies to market driven economies.

The hypothesis of this chapter is that a strategy in favour of financial liberalization in the emerging market economies of Central-East Europe will lead to Anglo-Saxon types of financial sectors, including the implantation of chronic short termism and vulnerability against speculative attacks. For economic policy we argue therefore in favour of a careful rehabilitation approach of existing institutional structures within transition economies.

This result is derived from theoretical reflections on the interrelationship of financial systems and economic development at the micro- and macroeconomic level, which are the first and the second part of this introduction. In the following section on the macroeconomics of financial systems we can unfortunately not resolve the jigsaw puzzle of finance and development, but find strong support for the 'Rhenish' system, which has the ability of building up hidden reserves in order to buffer intertemporal fluctuations of the business cycles. This finding is sufficient to support the adoption of a 'Rhenish' type of model for a strategy of the transition of financial sectors in Central-East Europe.

However, the third section will show, that Central-East Europe's situation is best characterized as a 'worst case scenario' of a mix-up between both models. Due to the unresolved bad asset problem of the past we find an apparent German system on the surface at the institutional level, but extreme short termism in the structural depth of the markets. This transitional phenomenon is a clear indicator of the economic system's ongoing transformation. The discussion of rehabilitation versus a 'free entry' approach will lead to the conclusion, that 'free entry' is an inappropriate policy for the promotion of sound financial sectors as long as the bad asset problem is not resolved. On the basis of this analysis our chapter will conclude in favour of a strategy of 'semi-liberalization', in order to use foreign participation to induce learning without giving away financial control.

1.1   Microeconomy: The dilemma of corporate governance theory

Most approaches to transition economics discuss the choice between an Anglo-Saxon type and a German type of financial system in terms of agency problems, and end up in a dilemma. Capital markets have been established, but do not yet perform as a market for corporate control. Banks, often set up as finance departments of firms and burdened with bad debts, show a questionable solvency and are prone to moral hazard (for an overview see Grosfeld, 1994). These weaknesses of the financial system can be weighted, whereby parts of finance and corporate governance theory are chosen to assess, whether a capital-based or bank-based should be followed. Policy advice always highlights the role of monitoring, screening and restructuring of insolvent firms and emphasizes either the role of banks or the role of capital markets for external funding and control. Even if proposals for the way ahead diverge, a contribution of the other, less pronounced part, be it banks or capital markets, is not denied. We suspect that this minor part shall fulfil a corrective function when, after a circular argument, the call for the principal's principal is not answered. Straightforward policy advice therefore seldom follows.

This unsatisfactory result of applied economic research is not as surprising as it may seem. The traditional way of gaining insights into the role of institutions has to be reversed, because in the case of the transition economy the focus is on building up institutions rather than explaining a given set. New institutional economics, the introduction of transaction costs and its incorporation into the theory of finance is a successful scientific programme, which explains the variety of existing institutions in developed market economies by their contribution to reducing the costs of controlling and enhancing contracts. It helps to assume that the existing institutions must be efficient and reduce transaction costs, otherwise they would have perished in a competitive environment. Giving policy advice for institution-building is a rather different research programme, especially when faced with institution-building in a transition economy, which by its nature, is in a process of revolutionary change. A range of efficient institutions does not yet exist and implemented or evolved institutions have interdependent effects on each other. Here the premature state of corporate governance theory for an application in transition economics becomes apparent. In spite of some eclectic arguments the interaction of institutions is still puzzling. Even if the countries concerned try to imitate Western systems, in what the term 'choice' suggests, they can only adapt singular institutions as parts of these systems. Therefore institution-building in transition economies will include a spontaneous process of trial and error.

1.2 Macroeconomy: Empirical arguments

Attempts have been made to integrate the theory of finance and macroeconomics (for example, Bernanke and Gertler, 1989 or Greenwald and Stiglitz, 1993), but these approaches are not applied to a comparison of financial systems. Empirical research might offer another argument for policy advice. Some cross-country studies demonstrate a correlation between stockmarket development and growth. This suggests that an Anglo-Saxon type of system with equity finance as the dominant form of external finance is better for development. But this relationship has to be viewed cautiously. Whereas rising credit at least means more intermediation, albeit not necessarily for productive means, rising equity prices need not reflect external funding in the form of new emissions on the primary stockmarket. It can be a reflex of internal accumulation or just a consequence of profit expectations. Moreover, a flow analysis by Corbett and Jenkinson (1997) shows that companies in the US and in the UK were the net financier on the stockmarket during the 1980s. Debt or profits have been used to buy previously issued shares back instead of being used to invest. In other words, a disinvestment/disintermediation took place with regard to the stockmarket. This was not the case in the emerging market economies of the Far East: there, new equity issues were the dominant source of external finance and contributed much more to corporate growth than in developed countries (Singh and Hamid, 1992). But this was partly due to regulation and tax advantages favouring stockmarkets. More importantly: a substitutive relationship between both kinds of external financing seemed to exist; stockmarket development fostered by international diversification did not coincide with growth but with domestic consumption and declining bank credit (Singh, 1997).

A recent controversy on finance and development (*Economic Journal*, 1997, Vol. 107) can be summarized as follows:

1. a correlation between financial development (intermediation as percentage of GDP) and economic growth cannot be denied; yet the question of causality still remains open;
2. the results of liberalization are disappointing;[1]
3. the statistics show different pictures for individual countries.

Unfortunately, no empirical argument in favour of a bank- or financial market-based financial system is stated. Arestis and Demetriades (1997, p. 785) put it in a general way: 'the causal link between finance and growth is crucially determined by the nature and operation of the financial institutions and policies pursued in each country.' In general, cross country studies cannot capture these differences. They argue in favour of time series analyses for each individual country separately. For transition economies there remain reservations against this method, because the time span under observation is still rather short.

2　Macroeconomics of financial systems

2.1　An anatomy of financial systems

In order to highlight differences between the Anglo-Saxon and German types of financial market the following arguments focus on external finance, although we admit that internal finance is the main source of investment in both systems. But having emphasized factors and macroeconomic groupings (low real exchange rate, income deflation combined with profit inflation see, for example, Hölscher, 1997), which foster internal finance, this focus can be misinterpreted as an aim to reverse the evolution of capitalism, characterized by a separation of ownership and control. Pure profits which reflect a flow disequilibrium are not considered.

Using the microeconomic arguments and the empirical results we interpret the difference between the Anglo-Saxon and German types of financial system as availability and use of long-term finance for investment. The main difference between both systems is the fact that in the German system, banks provide long-term finance in the form of credits to firms, whereas in the Anglo-Saxon type, long-term finance is provided by the capital market via equity. These basic assumptions characterize the prototypes. The reason for this difference can be found in the historical development, in particular the evolutionary process of specializing market participants and regulation or strong competition on the liability side of banks.

From a process-oriented viewpoint, the transformation of maturities is different. In Anglo-Saxon systems the transformation of maturities takes place on the capital market. Commercial banks offer short-term finance to firms with investment opportunities which decide after the investment has taken place, whether to refinance the initial amount by issuing shares (Chick, 1995). The firms therefore hold the transformational risk; liquid capital markets can reduce it and extend the flexibility of finance in principle. In the German system the banks have to bear the transformational risk and the 'golden banking rule' expresses the individual reduction of risk. Typically banking supervision controls the relationship of short-term liabilities and long-term assets in addition to restricting the danger of systemic risk. In both systems the initial source of finance is represented by bank credit.

The flexibility of bank credits might be welcome because it can provide purchasing power to the Schumpeterian entrepreneur, but it inherits the risk of inflationary pressure if too much money is created via bank credits and not transformed. Keynes for example mentions in the General Theory that the transformation of short-term into long-term finance is one factor that neglects the traditional link from the initial amount of money supply to prices. In addition, if the solvency of banks is in doubt the system inherits the risk of financial instability through the possible occurrence of bank runs (Diamond and Dybvig, 1983). In fact, both have been a major problem in Central-East Europe.

2.2 Reflections of different financial systems

Similar to the different finance option available for firms, households in either prototype are offered distinct asset options. In a monetary equilibrium created money has to be held deliberately in the portfolio of investors. Without internal finance the level of production is determined by the volume of assets that can be used for productive means. On the basis of simple anatomy a first conclusion could be that the Anglo-Saxon system offers a relative advantage over the German system if inflation expectations are the main obstacle to the economy concerned. Yet equity does not represent an absolute inflation secure asset. In a fixed exchange rate system rising prices lower the international competitiveness of the economy and reduced profit expectations stop share prices rising in line with inflation. Moreover inflation expectations can go hand in hand with the expectation of a future restrictive monetary policy, with a negative effect on share prices. Nevertheless equity seems to be more inflation secure than nominal assets. On the other hand the German system might offer a relative advantage if asset uncertainty is the main obstacle, because banks pool projects intersectorally. Although this function can be performed through a capital market that covers all sectors of the economy, it is rather doubtful that the individual investor really participates in all assets. Moreover, if small firms are not represented on the capital market even diversified investors unproportionally bear the risk of larger companies.

The description above does not capture some important dynamic differences between both systems. Let us consider rising profit expectations in an Anglo-Saxon economy. If these coincide with rising share prices a wealth effect leads to higher overall wealth and changes the relative distribution of assets for households, but without additional external finance for the firms in the first instance. The wealth effect restricts the expansion of the level of production in comparison with the German system because households have an incentive to rearrange their distribution of assets towards real or foreign assets. The opposite is true for depressed profit expectations. In support of this argument Black and Moersch (1998) find that the real exchange rate and the real interest rate show a negative correlation with investment for the German type of economies whereas in the Anglo-Saxon system there is none. This leaves us with a simple policy advice. So far as this is due to the wealth effect of the share prices it can be argued that the German type of system is favourable in prosperous macroeconomic situations, in which the advantages of an exchange rate strategy can be fully exploited. This preliminary result has to be taken cautiously. A recent study of the Bank for International Settlement (BIS) came up with the result that monetary policy in Anglo-Saxon systems is more effective.

Finally, one important difference between both systems has been emphasized by Allen and Gale in a number of articles. It is related to the described portfolio effects but emphasizes the welfare aspects. In the German system banks build up reserves in good times and draw on reserves in bad times (see also Frowen and Karakitsos, 1999). As a consequence they offer their creditors nearly the same pay-outs. The capital market in contrary cannot smooth the intertemporal risk in the same way. It cannot differentiate between an investor who is concerned with asset uncertainty because of a liquidity orientation and an investor who is concerned with profit arbitrage. Therefore, once the system is running and reserves are built up, the German system can make everybody better off. This intertemporal insurance for households has an obligatory character: direct investment facilities provided by a liberalized capital market offer arbitrage opportunities and undermine this feature. A larger set of alternatives, that is, markets plus financial intermediaries, might not make individuals better off than intermediaries alone (Allen and Gale, 1995, p. 190) – a statement in high contrast to most advice given to transition economies. With regard to transition economies, the immediate problem is not to build up reserves, but to smooth the write-off of the inherited bad debts over time.

3   The Central East European Scenario[2]

3.1   Bad debts and financial institutions

The major obstacle that the financial sectors of transition economies have in common is that these sectors are still burdened with a high proportion of bad assets in their balance sheets. (For an overview see Hölscher, 1998.) Only in the case of Hungary, where privatization of the financial sector was successfully finalized by massive state aid and other measures does this problem seem to be resolved. The Czech Republic is still shattered by the 1997 banking crises and Poland has seen many delays in attempts to privatize its financial sector.

Although the picture of financial sectors in transition economies shows diversity, general observations on an institutional level can be made. The absence of institutional investors like pensions funds leaves the emerging capital markets in a fragile condition in terms of transaction volume and number of market participants. As a consequence of restructuring policy, the overall picture shows the Rhenish style universal banking system. The structure of the financial market is oligopolistic, which alone would lead to rent-seeking behaviour with a higher lending rate than necessary. There are still very few well-equipped bank offices that offer the full range of financial services. Systems of clearing and payments are inefficient and slow; geographical differences are enormous. Apart from the capitals the CEECs are still 'underbanked' and suffer from huge disproportion in household deposit collections in the countryside and lending in the centres.

We find a combination of universal banking and high interest rate spreads, both as a result of restructuring. Yet universal banking alone is hardly the criterion for a German type of financial system. The refinancing structure of the banks shows the Anglo-Saxon feature of short-term liabilities, but due to the bad-debt problems monetary policy is not as effective. In short: Central-East Europe seems to be the worst case scenario as a mixture of both systems.

3.2   Rehabilitation versus liberalization

In the three East European countries attempts were made to separate the problem of bad assets from the problem of privatization of the enterprises that represent these bad assets. This went along with the improvement of the capital basis by consolidation bonds or privatization.

The state still holds a huge stake in the financial sector. Meanwhile all countries have introduced special state banks, with the task of collecting the 'bad assets' of the commercial banks. This rather new policy rejects the previous idea of a revenue-oriented privatization of state banks. The burden of the increasing indebtedness of the state as a consequence of this new move has to be balanced against the benefits of a functioning financial sector.

Another observation is the increasing number of joint ventures with foreign institutions throughout Central-East Europe. At a first sight this is a clearly optimistic sign, because it indicates the 'marketization' of the financial sectors. However, it could be regarded as a consequence of the hopeless attempts to set up domestic financial markets.

As the empirical picture clearly underlines the necessity of the reform of the banking system, the question is, which approach should be followed. A discussion of this question usually distinguishes between a *new entry* or *rehabilitation* strategy (see Claessens, 1996). The countries under observation obviously pursue a rehabilitation strategy even though 'choosing the rehabilitation approach strategy when faced with a weak institutional legacy can thus be a poor policy as progress is slow' (Claessens, 1996, p. 21). The alternative to such a 'poor policy' would be to set up a new financial sector with the help of foreign institutions. This would provide a solution for the flow functions of the system, but as the stock problem causes the major macroeconomic problem of the economies, this phenomenon also has to be addressed. Given all other conditions as equal, the new entry approach calls for a higher tax rate.

Instead of the banks, the state would have to take over in one form or another the burden of the bad assets.

Lessons from financial repression teach us that financial reform and liberalization may lead to 'an explosion in government debt, economic instability and lower economic growth' (Fry, 1997, p. 768) without fiscal reform incorporating either a reduction of government spending or increased tax revenue. Neither of these possibilities seem to be a realistic policy under the fragile circumstances of the transition economies. Therefore the new entry approach in the Visegrad countries would most likely initiate a return to the inflationary phase of the beginning of transition. This could even destroy growth and introduce political instability.

The alternative of the rehabilitation approach assumes growth as a necessary condition. If the economies are growing it is justified to introduce a strategy wherein bad debts are written off by the quasi-rents of the banking sector. The higher the quasi-rent, the faster the progress. Most important in this scenario are profit expectations of the entrepreneurial sector. A Schumpeterian strategy would allow a higher lending rate as long as profit expectations of entrepreneurs are high enough to increase investment. This policy option builds on factor augmentation rather than on factor allocation (see also Hölscher, 1997).

Of course this approach does not say anything about the improvement of inefficient allocation of savings and distribution of lending. But from a macroeconomic point of view it is sensible to separate this problem from the transition of the banking sector as such, rather than to externalize it to new entry candidates. The aim must be to prevent the creation of new bad loans, which are not a consequence of the past, but a consequence of bad management. This situation calls for a tough supervision system together with a proper accounting system. Recent banking failures show a backwards movement, because the new bankrupt banks in the Czech Lands are again under the direct supervision of the Nationalbank, a trend back to the monobank.

The financial sector is still in its infant state in Central-East Europe due mainly to the bad asset problem, but also to other distortions. The conventional 'infant industry argument' applies to the banking sector in transition, although List's theory is not explicitly used here. Until the circle of 'bad assets–privatization–negative value' is broken, a solution for a sound financial sector will not be in sight. The alternative, to leave the old institutions to their own fate and start from scratch with newcomers, who would mainly come from outside, ignores the destabilizing effects of the existing distortions.

4 Conclusion: In favour of semi-liberalization

On the basis of the above discussion we argue in favour of a careful rehabilitation with foreign participation. This suggests a policy option in between the two radical solutions of 'free entry' and full rehabilitation. The following diagram summarizes the different policy options for the restructuring of the banking system and demonstrates the crucial link between a liberalization strategy and the bad debt solution.

A flow solution of the bad debt problem seems only to be feasible without a far-reaching liberalization. CEE banks with bad assets are less competitive than new or foreign institutions, because they cannot offer competitive rates. Therefore the rebuilding of the bad debts must have an obligatory character; it does not allow for new competitors. Direct investment facilities provided by a liberalized capital market also offer arbitrage opportunities and undermine the feature of intertemporal smoothing. A flow solution of the bad asset problem calls for a German type of financial system with the additional opportunity to exploit favourable macroeconomic situations. Economic growth is necessary to write off the bad debts. In view of the lack of a banking history the typical arguments in favour of a full rehabilitation strategy, which builds on local knowledge and an existing link between the banking and productive sector, look quite weak. Instead, joint ventures in the banking sector may lead to a contribution of foreign capital and management experience within this process. However, foreign investors will only contribute if the profit expectations are really high.

Within an Anglo-Saxon system of liberalized capital markets a flow solution of the bad asset problem is not feasible. Even if the domestic

	level of liberalization			
bad debt solution	*rehabilitation*	*joint ventures with banks*	*capital market liberalization*	*free entry*
state solution	domestic German type	German type	(domestic) Anglo-Saxon type	Anglo-Saxon type; failures of domestic banks likely
flow solution	domestic German type	German type	feasibility doubtful, danger of banking crises	not feasible

Figure 2.1 Liberalization and bad debt solution

capital market takes over the role of funding for investment and the banks' role is restricted to offer payment facilities a banking crisis is very likely to occur. Sooner or later the bad debts end up on the state's balance sheet. Free entry for foreign banks and foreign competition would show an immediate effect. Most important is that a liberalization of the capital market is a precondition for the development of a financial system because banks lose the ability of building up hidden reserves in order to buffer the intertemporal fluctuations of the business cycle.

Notes

1 In particular developing countries suffered the experience known as 'good-bye financial depression, hello financial crash'.
2 For a wide-ranging study on economic development in Central-East Europe see Hölscher *et al.* 1993–96.

References

Allen, F. and Gale, D. (1994) Limited Market Participation and Volatility of Asset Prices, *American Economic Review*, 84, 933–55.

Allen, F. and Gale, D. (1995) A Welfare Comparison of Intermediaries and Financial Markets in Germany and the US, *European Economic Review*, 39, 179–209.

Arestis, P. and Demetriades, P. (1997) Financial Development and Economic Growth: Assessing the Evidence, *Economic Journal*, 107, 442, 783–800.

Bernanke, B. and Gertler, M. (1989) Agency Costs, Net Worth, and Business Fluctuations, *American Economic Review*, 79, March, 14–31.

Black, S. and Moersch, M. (1998) Financial Structure, Investment and Growth, in S. Black and M. Moersch (eds), *Competition and Convergence in Financial Markets. The German and Anglo-American Models*, North Holland: Elsevier Science.

Bockelmann, H. (1996) Unterschiede in den nationalen Finanzstrukturen und ihre makroökonomische Bedeutung, in D. Duwendag (ed), *Finanzmärkte, Finanzinnovationen und Geldpolitik*, Schriften des Vereins für Socialpolitik, Neue Folge, vol. 242, Berlin.

Chick, V. (1995) *Finance and Investment in the Context of Development: A Post Keynesian Perspective*, DP 95–13, University College London, Department of Economics.

Claessens, S. (1996) *Banking Reform in Transition Countries*. The World Bank, Policy Research Working Paper, no 1642, Washington, DC.

Corbett, J. and Jenkinson, T. (1997) How is Investment Financed? A Study of Germany, Japan, The United Kingdom and the United States, *The Manchester School Supplement* 65, 69–93.

Diamond, D. W. and Dybvig, P. H. (1983) Bank Runs, Deposit Insurance and Liquidity, *Journal of Political Economy*, 91, 3, June, 401–19.

Frowen, S. and Karakitsos, E. (1999) Monetary Policy in the UK and Germany Under Conditions of Gobalised Money and Capital Markets: Lessons for the Personal Sector and Ethical Considerations, in F. Frowen and F. McHugh (eds),

(2000), *Risk, Financial Competition and Moral Responsibility*, London and New York: MacMillan Press/St. Martin's Press.

Fry, M. J. (1997) In Favour of Financial Liberalisation, *Economic Journal*, 107, 442, 754–70.

Gerschenkron, A. (1962) *Economic Backwardness in Historical Perspective: A Book of Essays*, Cambridge, MA.: MJT Press.

Greenwald, B. and Stiglitz, J. (1993) Financial Market Imperfections and Business Cycles, *Quarterly Journal of Economics*, 108, February, 77–114.

Grosfeld, I. (1994) *Financial Systems in Transition: Is There a Case for a Bank Based System?*, London: Centre of Economic Policy Research, Discussion paper, 1062.

Hölscher, J. (1997) Economic Dynamism in Central-East Europe: Lessons from Germany, *Communist Economies & Economic Transfomation*, 9, 2, 173–81.

Hölscher, J., Jacobsen, A., Tomann, H. and Weisfeld, H. (eds) (1993–96), *Bedingungen ökonomischer Entwicklung in Zentralosteuropa – Conditions of Economic Development in Central and Eastern Europe*, vols. 1–5, Marburg. Metropolis.

Myers, S. C. and Majluf, N. S. (1984) Corporate Financing and Investment Decisions when Firms have Information that Investors do not have, *Journal of Financial Economics*, 13, 187–221.

Schumpeter, J. A. (1911) *Theorie der wirtschaftlichen Entwicklung*, Münich: Duncker and Humblodt.

Singh, A. (1997) Financial Liberalisation, Stockmarkets and Economic Development, *Economic Journal*, 107, 442, 771–82.

Sing, A. and Hamid, J. (1992) *Corporate Financial Structures in Developing Countries*, International Finance Corporation Technical Paper, 1.

Steinherr, A. and Huvenirs, C. (1994) On the Performance of Differently Regulated Financial Institutions: Some Empirical Evidence, *Journal of Banking and Finance*, 18, 2, 271–306.

Tomann, H. (1997) Options to Resolve the 'Bad Asset Problem', in S. Frowen and J. Hölscher (eds), *The German Currency Union of 1990 – A Critical Assessment*, London/New York: Macmillan Press, St Martin's Press.

II
Russia

3
August '98 as a Turning Point of Russian Reforms

Vladislav Semenkov

The present financial crisis is widely recognized as the most severe one since the beginning of the Russian reforms. It started with a chain of smaller financial shocks from autumn 1997 culminating in August '98 with the collapse of short-term state obligations (GKO-OFZ pyramid), *de facto* default on internal and external debts, and drastic devaluation of the rouble.

Immediate consequences of the crisis were significant financial losses by many economic agents, domestic and foreign; temporary paralysis of the banking system; cessation of external credit for Russian companies and the state; drastic decline of production in the legitimate sector; unemployment growth – in particular among the highly qualified and enterprising; significant decline in real income and standard of living. The scale of these consequences has shattered the public confidence which has divided current history of Russia into periods 'before' and 'after' the 'Black August'.

Not all economic, political and social implications of the crisis took clear shape, but it brought to power the Primakov government, which immediately declared the change in goals, priorities, ways and means of economic policy to save Russian reforms. Primakov's 'New Deal' reflects a remarkable shift in public opinion and a shift towards more active state intervention in the economy. At the same time waves of criticism, mainly in the academic and business worlds, emerged trying to answer two traditional Russian questions: 'Who is to blame?' and 'What to do?'

1   First, who is really to be blamed not only for this particular crisis but for disorientation of the Russian reforms which paved the way for the financial crisis of 1997–98?

The ardent proponents of liberalism 'without frontiers' try to blame the previous governments and the Central Bank of Russia (CBR) for deviations from liberalism and monetarism. 'Contrary to widely prevailing opinion the policy pursued by Russian authorities was not liberal, nor strictly speaking reformist', insists A. Illarionov, Director of the Institute of Economic Analysis.[1] He sees the roots of the financial crisis in excessive budget outlays (social expenditures first of all) and wrong actions by the government, CBR and IMF and he concentrates on technicalities of finance, credit and currency management during the crisis. A significant part of this criticism can be accepted: belated devaluation of the rouble, low quality of management of the state debt composition, etc.

Speaking about the Central Bank's credit and exchange policy during the last three years, Illarionov calls it 'highly irresponsible'. While currency assets of the money authorities in the period from the introduction of the 'currency corridor' on 6 July 1995 until the last phase of the financial crisis in Summer 1998 were increased by merely 7.5 per cent, the main money aggregates in roubles grew by 135 to 155 per cent, and the nominal value of state securities by nearly 12 times. One has to agree that the emerging 'scissors' between currency assets and rouble liabilities made the rouble devaluation in August 1998 absolutely inevitable.

There are many explanations why rouble devaluation was delayed for so long. An official point was that it would bring back high inflation and with it social unrest. But this was disputed by independent experts who insisted that the government and CBR just tried to save the top Russian banks from bankruptcy. This looks more plausible if we take into account that the Russian banking system was supported by government subsidies in the period of high inflation and when the situation changed Russian banks had to rely on a massive attraction of foreign credits and on increasing their external indebtedness.

In 1993–94 the foreign assets and liabilities balance of the Russian banking system was kept close to zero. But from 1995 it steadily and increasingly became negative. In 1997 this negative balance doubled and achieved $21 bn. By the end of the year total currency liabilities were up to $32.3 bn – close to one-third of total bank assets. In the first half of 1998 these foreign liabilities were cut by $3 bn but it was not enough to avoid a 'zone of danger'. The rouble devaluation increased the currency liabilities of the banking system, a multiple rate of exchange fall bringing many important Russian banks to bankruptcy – this happened in August–September 1998.

Unlike two previous crises, the currency crisis of 1997–98 was not unavoidable. In the period between 1995 and 1997 there was an unprecedented boom of foreign investment in Russia. In 1997 alone, massive direct and portfolio (mainly!) investments were above $34 bln (7.6 per cent of the official GDP, or 11.3 per cent of the legitimate GDP). According to the MTS index, stock prices of Russian companies for nine months of 1998 grew by 3.5 times. Real annual returns of GKO-OFZ dropped from 130 to 140 per cent in Summer 1996 to 9 to 10 per cent in June–October 1997. This situation could lead to economic development and/or massive inflation. Both didn't happen because this money were just 'eaten' (or stolen?).

Those who had long opposed the liberal model of the Russian transition after 'Black August' received the most convincing evidence for their criticism and gained more credit from the Russian public and authorities. They trace the roots of the crisis much deeper. They regard the present financial crisis as a direct result of the primitively perceived monetarist policy of financial stabilization and liberalization for its own sake, which brought about a unique example of a national economy where the financial and credit sector is increasingly separated from production in the real sector.

The real sector itself is divided on privileged export-oriented industries (oil and gas, raw materials, metallurgy) and 'underdogs' which mainly produce for domestic consumption. The latter employ nearly half of the real sector labour, pay around 40 per cent of fiscal payments but receive only 20 per cent of all investments. These two elements of the real sector interact poorly and in fact belong to different economic spaces.

The mechanism of this disintegration was launched in 1992 by 'gaidaronomics', which proclaimed that after liberalization the only way to galvanize the investment process and economic growth is eradication of inflation at any price. This price turned out to be the destruction of the economy and the degradation of Russian society.

From this point of view, bringing down the level of inflation to 11 per cent in 1997 (against 21.8 per cent in 1996) was interpreted as an 'opening of the era of economic stabilization and sustainable growth'. In fact, open inflation was transformed into hidden inflation[2] by the growth of arrears, debts, delays in salaries and wage payment etc. So called 'economic growth' was achieved by including part of the 'shadow' production into official statistics (see interview with head of Economic

Department of the Presidential Administration Dr Danilov-Danilian, Expert 15.09.97, p. 14).

Apart from this, from 1992 the so called 'stabilization process' was accompanied by unprecedented decline of production which resulted in a fall of the GDP by 50 per cent, industrial production by 60 per cent, agriculture – by 40 per cent and investments by 85 per cent. A significant part of production capacity was destroyed and functioning enterprises saw a universal slump in their rate of return.

By the beginning of 1998 the share of loss-making enterprises in the real sector of economy achieved 50 per cent; profits and depreciation funds of the other half of these enterprises did not provide normal conditions for extended reproduction and sometimes even for simple reproduction. On 1 October 1998, 49.7 per cent of the total number of enterprises and organizations were loss-makers (51.4 per cent in industry, 42.4 per cent in construction, 58.5 per cent in transport).[3] The rate of return in industry was 5.2 per cent and the profit rate in the real sector (industry, transport and communication) dropped to 7.4 per cent.[4] Depreciation funds were mainly used for replenishment of working capital to prevent a total collapse of production. Working capital formation was provided mainly by arrears for delivered good and only 2 per cent by cash from balance accounts of enterprises and organizations.

It is well known that profits and accumulated depreciations are the main source of financial resources for investment. Achievement of 'financial stabilization' in 1997 was accompanied by drastic constriction of the financial components of reproduction in the real sector of the national economy. In its turn this constriction contributed to the deep and lasting payment crisis. In January 1998, total accounts payable (on banks credits and loans) of enterprises in industry, construction, transport and agriculture were 1453.0 bn. roubles, including 782.2 bn roubles as arrears (29.2 per cent of GDP). Compare this latter with receivables – 17.1 per cent – and it becomes clear that real sector enterprises were heavily in debt.

The situation was aggravated by the fact that there were four payment instruments operating in the country: old and new roubles, foreign exchange, surrogates and barter, altogether exceeding GDP. Barter share varied from 45 per cent to 80 per cent.[5] In fact, the total economy where possible switched to non-money forms of payment and to shadow operations where the 'black cash' was helpful for tax evasion.

A direct consequence of the dramatic financial situation in the real sector was a debt crisis in the state financial system. Notwithstanding the increased number of taxes introduced in 1997 the planned volume of budget income proved unattainable. On the contrary, arrears on tax payments to the federal budget by December 1997 increased by 1.7 times from the start of 1996. In absolute terms, on 1 January 1998 the total of arrears to the budgets of all levels reached 162.3 bn roubles, that to the federal budget alone being 73.3 bn roubles. Hence the huge deficit in the state budget despite significant cuts in government spending.

Accumulation of tax arrears led to a situation where actual tax collections are regularly below the level of charged taxes. The economic nature of a significant part of tax arrears has much in common with the virtual nature of the Russian economy. In essence, these are virtual (fictitious) taxes, charged on virtual (fictitious) produce. Therefore notwithstanding any efforts of tax authorities the main part of tax arrears is hardly collectable, because it is charged on non-existent real values. It is not associated with any produce nor with any value added.

Steady reduction of budget income led to the necessity of borrowing in the internal securities market and after 1995 this resulted in a rapid growth of the domestic state debt. By the middle 1998 domestic debt reached 25.6 per cent of GDP. It promoted the growth of expenditure for debt service. By 1998 this had become one of the largest outlays of the state budget. In 1996 it amounted to 4.8 per cent of GDP and in the first half of 1998 to 3.9 per cent.[6]

At the same time large scale borrowing on the external financial markets was launched. As a result, by the beginning of 1998 debt service alone exceeded 30 per cent of all budget expenditures (82 bn roubles for internal obligations and $12 bn for external).

When state borrowings demanded much more resources than the volume of internal liquidity savings the decision to let non-residents operate on the state internal debt market was taken. In April 1998, according to the Ministry of Finance, non-residents' share of the market was about 28 per cent. Temporarily it helped to reduce interest rates and thus improve the state debt-service situation but made national finances more vulnerable to attacks by international speculators.

Forcing Russia to greater integration into the world economy the ruling regime did not make sufficient provision for national economic security. The country, where GDP is only $445.8 bn (1997), is increasingly open to the global financial system where the daily volume of currency transactions is above $1 trln. By 1998 the gates to this system were opened pretty wide.

In Russia in March 1998 there were 16 banks with 100 per cent foreign capital, 10 with a 50 per cent share and 145 with a smaller presence of foreign shareholders. Twelve foreign credit institutions applied for permission to open daughter companies. The share of foreign capital in the Russian bank system was estimated close to 8 per cent (by law the limit is 12 per cent). Also about 400 foreign banks were holders or traders of former Soviet debts to the London Club with total amount of $32.6 bn.

The West allowed Russian banks to extend their operations abroad. In January 1998 70 of these banks had 10 branches and 100 offices abroad. But this action had its negative side: by the end of 1997 total obligations of the Russian credit institutions abroad exceeded their assets by $6 bn. To compare – in Summer 1997 the figure was $2.5 bn and in 1996 their assets exceeded their liabilities by $0.5 bn. Non-resident share in Russian inter-banks credits increased in the beginning of 1998 to 60 per cent.[7]

As is evident, the increasing dependence of the Russian economy on external forces is manifested in different forms. But there are two main factors that interacted with the internal weakness of the economy and finally brought its financial and credit sector to a critical point. These factors are: 1. the excessive orientation of the balance of payments and currency reserves on energy and raw materials export; and 2. massive attraction of non-residents' resources to GKO market.

Under the present structure of Russian external trade the amount of currency and budget income of the country depends heavily on the world oil market which is highly volatile. In 1996 the oil price was high, $23 per barrel but by August 1998 it had fallen to $12 per barrel causing about $5 bn losses to the Russian oil industry. The 1998 budget was based upon very wrong estimates that oil prices would be kept at around of $18 to $20 per barrel.

But an even more serious mistake was the large-scale attraction of 'hot money' from abroad to the GKO market. As a result, by the end of 1997 non-residents controlled about 30 per cent of the GKO-OFZ portfolio. This mechanism works with two main conditions: 1. inflow of new resources to the market should exceed the amortization payments and the difference should go to the budget; and 2. amortization money should be reinvested into new issues and not escape from the market. Otherwise the whole pyramid has no sense – there are only expenses for amortization and currency for non-residents to expatriate their earnings.

The very concept of the GKO pyramid was strongly criticized from the very beginning by most respected Russian academic and business experts as a bonanza for national banks and international speculators at the expense of the state budget and collapsing economy. From 1993 to 1998 the government received from the state securities market

Rbl 32 bn. but spent Rbl 450 bn. to pay interest and amortization.[8] The short-term state papers became a sort of 'vacuum cleaner' for the scarce resources so much needed in the real sector.

The critics proved to be correct in other respects as well. With the first signs of the Asian financial crisis non-residents withdraw their 'hot money' to reinvest it in the less profitable but safer US market. From November 1997 to March 1998 non-residents evacuated from Russia about $3 bn per month. The total sum repatriated was close to $18 bn. and more than $10 bn were the receipts from state paper sales.[9]

The World financial crisis is the last event to be blamed for the Russian misfortunes. It acted as a catalyst for our own negative tendencies and mistakes. The whole system, built up on an artificial stability of rate of exchange and state debt market – both external and domestic – was fragile and vulnerable even to relatively small and remote shocks because it was 'virtual' by nature and far from real production and socioeconomic realities.

2 Second question to answer – What to do?

The August '98 crisis has drawn a line under earlier attempts at 'marketization' of the Russian economy. It was stressed many times both by domestic reformers and their advisers from abroad that the most advanced segment of the economy was the banking system.

On 1 December 1998 out of 2484 banks registered by CBR, 1496 were actually operating. Their authorized capital was Rbl 50 bn.[10] As of April 1998 the main financial sources of banks were juridical entities – 37 per cent. Population savings formed 5 per cent and budget resources only about 2 per cent.[11] This very fragile and unreliable basis was weakened after August '98 due to 'freezing' in GKO-OFZ about Rbl 40 to 50 bn of their net worth. In August 1998 the banking system was nearly dead, their capital shrunk by Rbl 13.5 bn and losses were Rbl 6.8 bn.

On 1 October seven banks out of the 25 largest lost all their capital and another 11 lost a significant part of theirs. Loss of trust in the banking system in general and in some banks in particular led to a freezing of operations on the inter-bank credit market.

CBR spent two months making a thorough analysis of the situation in the banking sphere and came to depressing conclusions: banks' net worth shortage was Rbl 72 bn, about half of all banks should be liquidated, about 200 needed support, 18 out of this number (so called 'system-building') need Rbl 47 bn. Others (mainly small and medium-sized regional and local banks) could survive.

A plan of actions was developed and the Agency for Restructuring of Credit Organizations (ARCO) was established by the government with its main task to work with assets of 'problem' banks by buying, value accretion, sales and utilization of earnings for restoration of liquidity of certain banks. Resources for banks' restructuring at only Rbl 30 bn are deemed to be inadequate.

E. Primakov proposed the creation of a special Bank of Reconstruction to restore macroeconomic stability, improve the investment climate and mobilize internal and external resources for credit to real sector enterprises. These measures are regarded by some experts as a strengthening of state governance in the financial sector with possible negative, as they deem, effects, like division of banks on 'good' state banks to pipe in resources to certain enterprises and 'bad' commercial banks which do not contribute to the rehabilitation of real sector and intend to make easy money again. Naturally clients will go to these new banks and it will be enterprises of the strategically important industries: fuel and energy complex, defence, metallurgy and communications. But what is wrong with it? The easy money times are over and those banks that wish to survive have to adapt themselves to new conditions, to learn more about industry investment policy, and to operate within the domestic financial system like real, not 'virtual', credit institutions. It is true that the present situation in the finance sector is far from normal. But the first shock is over and there are some positive signs. First, a tension caused by the end of the moratorium on external debt amortization has disappeared. There were expectations of legal actions against Russian banks, arrest of their accounts and property abroad and, as a result, further destabilization of financial markets. It did not happen. The Russian government statement that, in 1999, Russia is able to pay only $9 bn out of $17.5 bn debt did not arouse a strong negative reaction by Western investors. Quotations of the Russian currency debts did not change much. In fact, they grew up a little when an agreement on the restructuring of GKO was agreed in principle. In general, the level of prices on Russian currency debt are still very low. These securities earnings are at annual levels of 35 to 78 per cent and remain unchanged during the last three months. After adoption of the scheme for restructuring the GKO (10 per cent 'alive money'; 20 per cent non-coupon obligations, which permits the payment of tax arrears; and 70 per cent four and five-year coupon obligations) the next problem to be negotiated with non-residents is to determine possibilities and dates of conversion of 'alive' money received into hard currency.

A solution to all these problems would enable the Ministry of Finance to trade on MMVB with both old and new state securities. In the meantime the CBR tries to trade its obligations, but without much success. Weighted-average earnings of these papers is at an annual level of 41 per cent with daily volume around $3–4 mn. The CBR obligation market did not manage to replace habitual GKO-OFZ, did not fulfil the task of supporting banks' current liquidity and was unable to draw out any significant resources from the currency market.

There are rumours that soon new state securities will be traded on the Moscow Inter-bank Currency Exchange (MMVB). These securities have appeared as result of restructuring of GKO-OFZ. Experts have strong doubts about the success of this trading because it would be difficult to find investors to buy papers with low earnings and high risk.

There is still no sound view of the future of the financial market. At present 85 per cent of its composition belongs to the currency market. All others – stock market, bonds, inter-bank credits, bank debts – occupy only 15 per cent. Practically, an internal market for domestic currency loans does not exist. Opinion prevails that August '98 may become a turning point for the Russian stock market which had just completed its early stage of development. It needed the August shock to rid it of its two main disproportions: domination of foreign capital; and underdevelopment of market infrastructure which discouraged investments in the real sector.

In 1997 total capitalization of the corporate papers' market in Russia achieved $170 bn (against $50 bn in 1996). Though it was exclusively a 'virtual' growth not supported by economic growth in real sector, its return on foreign investments was around 10 per cent.

Foreign investors controlled more than 80 per cent of Russian 'blue chips' and stock instruments of second and third echelons. By world standards the rate of capitalization of security market in proportion to GDP in Russia was one of lowest – about 20 per cent (compared with 34 per cent in Mexico or 46 per cent in Brazil). On international stock exchanges 14 Russian joint-stock companies traded their stocks. At the same time there were 200 issuers from 40 000 privatized enterprises represented in the RTS. About 70 per cent of turnover was concentrated in a dozen papers, which is an eloquent comment on the rest of the stocks.

Loss of investors' trust of the Russian stock market plummeted with the high-priced shares of largest Russian corporations. A year ago most prospering Russian enterprises had a market value comparable with much stronger Western companies. Now they can be bought cheaply.

Only the very high investment risks prevent foreign 'bargain hunters' from immediately buying some of those which may later turn into a bonanza.

The total value of the 14 largest Russian industrial corporations included in 1997 in the list of 500 leading companies of Europe (FT rating) was by the end of October 1998 only $16 bn. A year earlier, in October 1997 their value was $114 bn or 7 times higher and the same year their profit was $20.8 bn. Russian shares are so cheap because nobody wants to buy them. It is like the popular story about cowboy Joe who is imperceptible because nobody is trying to catch him. There was an exodus of operators from the Russian stock market. Due to heavy losses and lack of trust in the future of the market they refused to pay their fees to RTS.

In October 1998 the Board of Directors ruled more than 100 organizations out of RTS. The volume of trades in third quarter of 1998 dropped by 80 per cent compared with the same period in 1997. In September it was $28.8 mn, in October $45.8 mn. Compare these figures with May 1998 when they stood at $70 mn. With the average size of brokerage between 0.1 and 0.3 per cent, in September–October 1998 the companies and banks earned about $150 000 which is not enough to pay salaries even to leading brokers – their main 'bread-winners'.[12]

The hard life makes some companies innovative in attempts to win the weakened Russian corporate market. 'Troika-Dialog' plans to transform RTS into a certain replica of the London Stock Exchange with a high rate of internationalization of stock trading by exploiting presently idle trading spots and introducing into RTS a system of index quoting of foreign issuers' securities (some of them from CIS).

The investment company 'Aton' tries to establish a special club for investors from the second echelon. Members of the club will be consolidated in a certain 'pool' which takes responsibility for the legal protection of its members in their disputes with the management of enterprises should they abuse shareholders' rights. An exotic operation of swapping shares between enterprises has been introduced on the stock market.

Optimism is prevailing among Russian participants with regard to the future of the stock market. It will be proved correct as soon as the Government starts its plans for the GKO amortization and new rouble emission. Cash flow will refill the financial market and roubles should be invested somewhere. The CBR will try to limit currency purchases but unusually cheap shares are available and they may bring a fortune very soon.

Partly the above mentioned optimism is based on an understanding that the August '98 shock did nothing else but equalize the situation between the financial and real sectors. Presently it is neither feasible nor desirable to return to the pre-August '98 position or to reanimate financial markets without rehabilitation of other sectors of the Russian economy.

The Primakov government is busy with emergency action to keep the economy alive and to avoid by any available means, including controlled emission and IMF credits, any social and political unrest. But a coherent and comprehensive anti-crisis programme of national salvation, a sort of 'Russian New Deal', is badly needed.

It looks like neither the Government, nor the liberals have this programme. But there are pilot projects proposed by experts from the Council of Federations[13] and economists from the Academy of Sciences[14] which are based upon principles of the so called 'mobilization' model.

Very briefly these principles are:

1 Mobilization of all non-fiscal sources of budget income (de-commercialization of CBR with transfer of all its profits to budget; introduction of state monopoly on export of gas, on import of alcohol and tobacco; increasing rent payments for exploitation of natural resources; improvement of management of state property).
2 Centralization of currency resources of the country, gradual de-dollarization of the banking system; reinforcement of curency control and regulation.
3 Strict control of price formation and operations in natural monopolies up to re-nationalization of some of them (on sound legal ground).
4 Re-nationalization of some bankrupt enterprises whose produce is essential for the normal operation of the national economy.
5 Re-orientation of money and credit policies towards production accompanied by adequate regulation of interest rates and money flow.
6 Radical suppression of organized crime and eradication of corruption of state bureaucracy.
7 Protection of rights of private and public property, promotion of competition and anti-monopoly control in commerce.
8 Adoption of measures of protection of domestic markets and stimulation of national products competitiveness.
9 Promotion of active industrial, structural and technological policy within limits set up by present critical situation.

It is clear that this plan of action most of all needs the political will and vision of our authorities. Some steps have been made but progress is slow. We are short of time and if not now then later much more radical measures will need to be taken: total nationalization of banks, natural monopolies and vital enterprises, 'closing' the country and maintain and enhance law and order by force.

Notes

1 *Voprosy Economiky*, 12, 1998, 20.
2 *Rossisky Econ. Zhurnal*, 5–6, 1995; 11–12, 1997.
3 *Nezavisimaya Gazeta-Politeconomia*, 20, December 1998, 10.
4 *Nezavisimaya Gazeta-Politeconomia*, 7–8, 1998, 4.
5 *Finansovye Izvestya*, 2 April 1998.
6 *Finansovye Izvestya*, 2 April 1998, 38.
7 *Finansovye Izvestya*, 2 April 1998.
8 *Finansovye Izvestya*, 9 June 1998.
9 *Finansovye Izvestya*, 11 June 1998.
10 *Nezavisimaya Gazeta*, 30 December 1998, 4.
11 *Finansovye Izvestya*, 23 April 1998, iii.
12 *Nezavisimaya Gazeta-Politeconomia*, 19, December 1998, 11.
13 *Rossisky Econom. Zhurnal*, 4, 10 1998.
14 *Voprosy Economiki*, 3, 1996.

4
What Happened to Russia? Comments on Vladislav Semenkov

Thomas Linne

Mr Semenkov's fundamental message is that the crisis proved the failure of the reform efforts. He takes it as an opportunity to recommend some drastic measures. I agree with Mr Semenkov that the crisis has created many problems. But we differ by a great deal on the envisaged way out of the crisis. I think the problems Russia is facing are managable and require more and deeper reforms.

We all know what happened in Russia in mid-August 1998. The government suspended payments on its internal and external debt while the central bank at the same time widened the exchange rate band and finally moved to a free float. So the question is: what went wrong? Russia's financial crisis did not appear overnight, but rather was the result of more fundamental problems. I want to focus on a few domestic factors which lead to the events in August 1998.

Fiscal policy

Russia's problem in financing its government spending was a symptom of some deeper problems. In particular, there was insufficient will on the government's side to impose hard budget constraints needed to pursue successful reforms. The government granted widespread tax exemptions to certain enterprises, it failed to pursue tax evaders vigourously, and it refused to apply the insolvency law aggressively enough. The availability of international financial aid allowed the government to postpone some of the tough measures necessary to balance the budget. Future fiscal policy requires a willingness by the government to enforce financial discipline in its own operations and for the enterprises. This will stimulate the fundamental micro-level restructuring that the missing soft budget constraints delayed. However, the

39

budget for 1999 – first one after the crisis – may again go in the wrong direction.

Weak banking sector

The importance of a sound banking sector to a healthy economy cannot be overstated. On the eve of the crisis many of the Russian banks – mainly Moscow based banks – were highly exposed to currency risk. The devaluation of the Rouble made their liabilities highly expensive, and the government default on its debt completely wiped out almost half of their assets. With more than half of the private banks being insolvent, the crisis is a golden opportunity to start afresh in building a financial system that can do the job Russia was lacking in the past. Namely, turning domestic savings into investment capital for viable enterprises. Key to a lasting solution of the banking crisis is the recapitalisation of banks under the condition that new losses can be prevented. Strengthening the banking supervision goes without saying. It was not good practice in the past to give away bank licences like lottery tickets. A step in the right direction is the recently passed insolvency law for credit institutions. Another step to restore confidence in the troubled banking sector is to remove existing entry barriers for foreign competition. The central bank's proposal for the restructuring of the banks bears some interesting aspects, but its greatest shortcoming is that it does not specify how the programme will be financed.

Exchange rate policy

The exchange rate policy turned out to be too restrictive to absorb external shocks. The exchange rate band would have provided sufficient room for a devaluation of the rouble prior to the crisis. But even the widening of the band in early 1998 failed to play a significant role as the central bank prevented a depreciation of the Rouble by interventions. So indeed, the central bank effectively pursued a fixed rate regime. The tying of monetary policy to the exchange rate target required high interest rates as a response to dwindling market confidence. As a result of falling inflation, real interest rates turned out to be prohibitively high to stimulate capital investment.

Prior to the crisis there has been growing discrepancy between a loose fiscal policy and a passive monetary policy which had created a vicious circle of rising fiscal deficits, high interest rates, the short-term roll-over financing strategy, and an ever growing interest burden on the budget.

What is necessary in the future is a tighter fiscal policy which is consistent with monetary policy. With a flexible exchange rate regime the central bank has regained sovereignty over its monetary policy. And with reduced budget deficits in the future there is a realistic chance to reconcile both policies.

Privatization vs competition

Mr Semenkov proposes some urgency measures including the re-nationalization of strategic and even viable enterprises. That is quite radical and sounds like turning back the clock. He suggests that state ownership of certain enterprises is superior to private ownership. Rather than changing ownership of enterprises the focus of economic policy should be directed towards setting the right incentives to foster competition.

Russia's privatization experience is perculiar: the huge rents created by privatization have encouraged entrepreneurs to try to secure privatized enterprises rather than invest in their own companies. Whereas in contrast, competition policy often undermines rents and creates incentives for wealth creation. Privatizing state monopolies has created powerful interests that have undermined the possibility of regulation or competition in the future (Stiglitz, 1998). The conclusion from the crisis should not be to suspend privatization or to re-nationalize enterprises but to create competition and, on the part of the state to provide the right incentives for the economic agents.

Concluding remarks

It is hard at this time to be optimistic about Russia. The pressures at the moment are all for government intervention in the form of spending and subsidies to circumvent the hardships of reform. Both reform and reformers seem to be discredited. The message from the events of August 1998 should be that the shortcomings have been due to too little reform rather than too much reform. And I do hope with Mr Semenkov that the crisis really turns out to be the turning point in Russia's reform efforts in the sense that the reforms will be speeded up, broadened and deepened.

References

DIW/IfW/IWH (1998) *Die wirtschaftliche Lage Rualands: Krise offenbart Fehler der Wirtschaftspolitik, Dreizehnter Bericht*, IWH Forschungsreihe, October.

DIW/IfW/IWH (1999) *Die wirtschaftliche Lage Rualands: Schuldenstreichung statt Reformen?, Vierzehnter Bericht*, IWH Forschungsreihe, March.
Stiglitz, J. E. (1998) More Instruments and Broader Goals: Moving Toward the Post-Washington Consensus, *WIDER Annual Lecture*, 2, Helsinki.

5
Comment on Vladislav Semenkov

Adalbert Winkler

1 Introduction

Professor Semenkov's paper touches upon many issues and presents many provocative thoughts. Most of the macroeconomic issues are taken up in Linne's comment, whose general thrust is entirely in accord with my own basic position. Indeed, Linne shows that Russia was unable to stabilize stabilization policy (Winkler, 1996), due mainly, but by no means exclusively, to its failure to limit budget deficits by enforcing payment of taxes while cutting expenditures in a responsible manner. In the end, fiscal policy won the 'game of chicken' against monetary and exchange rate policy (Dornbusch, 1991; Sargent, 1986).

In a certain sense, the diagnosis of policy inconsistency validates Professor Semenkov's criticism of the stabilization strategy followed by Russian economic policymakers, whom he characterizes – incorrectly, in my view – as 'monetarists' and as adherents of 'neo-liberalism'. But given what he criticizes and the essential nature of his recommendations for the future, it can be concluded that he sees the inconsistency of macroeconomic policy as an outgrowth of the attempt to achieve monetary stabilization, and thus that, in his view, the attempt to bring about monetary stability led to the crisis and, by extension, to the country's economic decline. Therefore, one can also surmise that Professor Semenkov does not attribute Russia's current problems to a failure of fiscal policy, and thus, in a broader sense, to a failure in the area of institution building and institutional development.

This is surprising because experience has shown that without fiscal-policy stabilization there can be neither growth nor development, not least because it will prove necessary again and again to counteract a lack of budgetary discipline with a monetary policy which, given the state of the real economy, is too restrictive. There is no reason to believe that Russia is 'different' in this respect. Indeed, Russia, like every other economy in the world, will find that, in a market-based system, the attempt to achieve growth without monetary stability is bound to fail, thus confronting policymakers sooner or later with the question of whether they should change their macroeconomic orientation or change the overall orientation of national economic policy, i.e. abandon the commitment to build a market economy. Semenkov's paper suggests that if Russia should find itself at this crossroads, he would tend to argue against retaining the basic commitment to market economics. For this reason, his diagnosis, and the therapy he proposes, must be rejected, although some aspects of his analysis, and of the remedy he suggests, are certainly worth discussing.

This is true particularly with regard to the financial sector and to financial sector policy, topics which Semenkov deals with extensively in his paper. But because presentation of a detailed analysis of the distortions in the financial sector and of the mistakes made by those responsible for financial sector policy would divert attention from his main point, which is that a fundamentally inappropriate macroeconomic policy has been pursued, Semenkov interprets the financial crisis solely as a symptom, and not as part of the cause, of Russia's economic problems. Thus, paradoxically, he echoes the interpretation put forth by most of the 'monetarists' and 'neo-liberals', whom he attacks with such fervour. I will examine this proposition and assess its validity in the light of certain key insights drawn from the modern theory of banking and finance.

2 The Russian crisis as part of the international financial crisis

2.1 Special characteristics of transactions in financial markets

Many discussions of the causes of the Russian crisis devote little or no attention to the financial sector, and in view of the problems that Russia faces in the area of macroeconomic and transition policies, this tendency to ignore the role of the financial system is perhaps understandable. At the same time, though, I find it surprising. After all, the macroeconomic dislocations with which Russia has had to contend since August 1998 – a dramatic decline in the external value of the local currency; high and rising inflation rates; widening budget deficits; and a deep recession – are not uniquely Russian problems. Indeed, since mid-1997 these same phenomena have also been observed in many other countries in which the macroeconomic environment, specifically as regards the conflict between fiscal and monetary policy, differs sharply from the one that has evolved in Russia. At the very least, this raises the question of whether one can in fact explain the current crisis in Russia – whose emergence is seen by many observers, including Semenkov, as having coincided with the onset of the financial crisis in August 1998 – solely in terms of the distinct set of macroeconomic parameters found in Russia.

Financial crises are by no means uncommon in the development process of economies. In fact, financial and banking crises occurred again and again in Western industrial countries in the nineteenth and early twentieth centuries, and over the last 20 years a substantial number of developing countries have also experienced such crises (Caprio, 1997; Mishkin, 1991, 1996). And in Russia, where the transition to a market economy has only been under way for about a decade, crisis-like developments in the financial markets are also not a new phenomenon, having occurred periodically since 1992. For example, there was the 'rouble shock' on 11 October 1994, when the rouble plummeted 27 per cent against the US dollar in a single day (Boven and Winkler 1995). And in August 1995, the overnight rate – the interest rate at which Russian banks lend each other central bank money – rose from 10 per cent to 83.3 per cent per month in a single day, precipitating a severe liquidity crisis in the Russian money markets (Boven *et al.*, 1995).

Financial markets are susceptible to crises because they are used by economic agents to carry out intertemporal transactions, i.e. transactions that are undertaken in the present but 'extend into' the future. This intertemporal quality gives rise to two problems:

- The monitoring problem. Are the funds that have been provided being utilized by the recipient for the purpose agreed with the lender/investor, or, if no specific purpose was agreed, are they being used in a 'wise' manner?
- The problem of maturity transformation. What conditions must be met in order for it to be possible to finance long-term investments with short-term funds?

2.2   A brief look at modern banking theory:
The models of Diamond (1984) and Diamond and Dybvig (1983)

Both problems have received a great deal of attention in the theory of financial intermediation. Diamond (1984) explains why, as institutions, commercial banks should be well equipped to solve the monitoring problem in an efficient manner. However, the model specifies certain implicit conditions which must be fulfilled in order for banks to be able to solve the monitoring problem in a satisfactory way:

- There must be no macroeconomic risks.
- Banks must be able to monitor (and/or analyse) borrowers.
- Banks must have diversified portfolios.
- The non-pecuniary costs which would have to be borne by a bank if it failed must be so high that they provide a sufficient incentive for it to monitor its borrowers.

Because this set of conditions, which must be met if the Diamond model is to work, cannot be assumed to be given in the real world, financial systems do not develop smoothly. They experience periodic crises, unless sound stabilization policies are implemented, banking supervision is efficient, and financial institutions have sound corporate governance structures (Winkler, 1997). It is amply apparent that since the beginning of the transition process, the Russian financial system has evolved in an environment in which none of these criteria are met. Thus, there would seem to be little doubt that the consensus view on the origins of the Russian crisis, namely that: macroeconomic stabilisation failed; that there were 'bad banks' and poor, inadequate banking supervision; and that there was a lack of transparency in financial markets, is correct. However, it tends to obscure the fact that even under vastly more favourable conditions than those found in Russia – in other words, even if banks perform their financial intermediation functions properly and even if the quality of banking supervision is satisfactory – the banking system will still experience periods of instability,[1] and this inherent instability is an outgrowth of the unique quality of financial intermediation as it is carried out by banks. Indeed, while banks – due to their monitoring activities and their ability to pool demands – are better providers of liquidity to borrowers than individual depositors (Rajan, 1996), this liquidity creation simultaneously confronts them with a problem which they cannot solve on their own. Specifically, if depositors wish to sell their deposits on a large scale, banks are unable to sell their assets in the market at a price which would allow them to repay their creditors (the depositors). The reason for this is quite simple: the real value of the banks' assets cannot be accurately assessed by the public because it has delegated the monitoring function to the banks (Goodhart, 1988). Accordingly, banks need a lender of last resort who is ready to provide them with liquidity in return for assets which are accepted as loan security in 'normal' circumstances (Bagehot, 1873).

That banks are inherently unstable institutions is demonstrated even more forcefully by the discussion of the problem of maturity transformation in Diamond and Dybvig (1983). They show that maturity transformation necessarily implies the risk of illiquidity at the aggregate level of the economy, regardless of how well financial institutions operate, because – by definition – 'a demand deposit contract which is not subject to runs provides no liquidity services.' (p. 409). Thus, Diamond and Dybvig also argue that there must be a lender of last resort[2] so that financial and banking crises can be prevented, thus enabling economies to reap the benefits of a dynamic, expanding banking system.[3]

2.3 Why was the August '98 crisis so severe?

As can be seen both from the empirical data and from a brief review of the pertinent theoretical contributions, it is by no means unusual for financial systems to experience crises, especially in countries in which radical political and economic changes have created an unstable overall environment. Thus, financial crises must be accepted as a fairly normal occurrence in a country like Russia. But if this is so, why has the latest one, which emerged in August 1998, proved to be so 'abnormal', so severe? Why has the crisis of 1998 turned out to be 'the big one', and what kept a crisis of similar magnitude and severity from occurring in 1994 or 1995?[4] The answer, I think, lies not only in the specific nature of the macroeconomic situation that had evolved in Russia, which is outlined briefly above, but also in the fact that the crisis of August '98 was a crisis in an international financial market, and not only in the Russian financial market (Stremme, 1998).[5] Specifically, this meant that, unlike in 1994, and in contrast especially to the situation in 1995, the Central Bank of Russia was unable to serve as the lender of last resort. The reason was very simple: depositors who wished to withdraw their funds from Russian banks did not want roubles, but rather hard currencies like the US dollar and the D-mark. And the CBR is no more able to provide funds to banks in hard currencies than are its counterparts in countries like Thailand, South Korea, Indonesia and Brazil.

However, in the absence of a lender of last resort, international investors find themselves in the same situation as the depositors in the Diamond and Dybvig model. So long as each individual in this group assumes that all of the other investors will not withdraw their DM- or US$-denominated deposits, it is advantageous for each of them, and for the group as a whole, to keep all funds on deposit. But if an individual investor is convinced that all of the other investors will withdraw their DM- or US$-denominated deposits, he will also withdraw his deposits because he knows that at the international level, in contrast to the situation in a national financial market, there is no central bank which can guarantee that US$ or DM deposits will be converted into cash in the form of dollars or D-marks. And if this is the prevailing view among international investors/depositors, it will have one of two effects: either a bank run will be precipitated or, if a run has already started, it will gain momentum and be even harder to stop, with the rush to remove funds taking the form of a run on the entire national financial system. Once this point has been reached, interest rate increases by the central bank have no impact: the high interest rate does not keep investors from withdrawing their money because they must assume that interest would not be paid on deposits if they were maintained.

It is surely correct to assume that such behaviour is not caused entirely by sunspots, in other words that it is also prompted by an assessment of economic fundamentals. Indeed, crisis-like developments have not occurred in all emerging markets, as is shown in the paper by Polañski (1999) which appears in this book, and those that have experienced crises have certainly not all suffered damage on the same scale. However, an interpretation of events that is grounded in modern banking theory leads one to question the view that the financial crises of recent years have been merely an outgrowth of more or less unique sets of macroeconomic problems in the various economies that have been affected. What it highlights instead is a systemic problem that appears to have had more or less the same effect on a range of countries – including Indonesia, South Korea, Russia and Brazil – whose economies, and the fundamental economic problems they face, differ significantly. The problem is as follows: in the absence of controls on international capital flows, and given the lack of an effective regulatory framework for cross-border investment transactions, modern international capital markets are forced to operate in much the same way as did national capital markets in the Western industrial countries in the nineteenth century in so far as they must do without a lender of last resort. Therefore, it is not surprising that the international financial system today appears to be susceptible to crises in much the same way as national financial systems were a hundred years ago, and that, in terms of the severity of their effects on real economic activity, modern international crises resemble the national financial crises of the nineteenth century. These similarities are particularly evident in cases where an attempt has been made to implement an exchange rate-based stabilization policy, that is, in cases where the exchange rate has been used as a nominal anchor.

3 Conclusions

In view of the points raised above, I certainly agree with Semenkov when he says that August 1998 marked a turning point in the process of economic reform in Russia. But my diagnosis of the causes of the crisis differs radically from his diagnosis, and my ideas on the kind of therapy that is needed if the process of economic decline is to be halted in Russia are also radically different from those that he advocates. Specifically, my interpretation of the events of August 1998 and their impacts on the real economy does not lead me to conclude that increased state intervention, particularly at the micro level (for example price controls, re-nationalization, state monopolies, re-orientation of monetary and credit policies to promote industrial production), is what Russia needs to resolve the crisis. The reason for this is quite simple. The crisis was not caused by developments at the micro level. Indeed, what happened in Russia in August 1998 indicates that a country cannot achieve monetary stability unless its fiscal policy is sound. But it also shows that if a country whose overall economic environment is unstable does not impose controls on capital inflows and outflows, especially short-term portfolio investment, and if it has also in effect adopted a policy of fixed exchange rates, the lack of controls on capital movements will sooner or later precipitate a crisis because there is no institution that would be both willing and able to act as a lender of last resort to stop a run on the national financial system by foreign investors.

Notes

1 See, for example, the two postwar episodes of financial turbulence in the United States which are described by Mishkin (1991, pp. 98 ff).
2 or, alternatively, a government deposit insurance scheme
3 In the Diamond and Dybvig model, the ability to exploit more productive investment opportunities is the main benefit offered by such a system.
4 Indeed, one must ask why the previous crises had just the opposite effect: they prompted renewed attempts to stabilize the economy which were effective in so far as Russia was able to keep its GDP, which had already fallen significantly, from declining still further – a substantial achievement, all things considered.
5 An international financial market is defined as the totality of the supply of and demand for financial assets denominated in a currency which is a foreign currency for one of the two sides (market participants of various nationalities). Accordingly, international financial markets are identical to national financial

markets, except for the implication that the currency basis for transactions is not the same.

References

Bagehot, W. (1873) *Lombard Street*, Homewood, II. Richard, D. Irwin Inc.

Boven, S. and Winkler, A. (1995) *After the Rouble Shock*, IPC Working Paper, 5, Frankfurt.

Boven, S., Soutchkov, S. and Winkler, A. (1995) *Liquidity Crisis in the Russian Money Markets*, IPC Working Paper, 7, Frankfurt.

Caprio, G. (1997) *Safe and Sound Banking in Developing Countries – We're Not in Kansas Anymore*, The World Bank, Working Paper, 1739, Washington, DC.

Diamond, D. (1984), Financial Intermediation as Delegated Monitoring, *Review of Economic Studies*, 51, 393–414.

Diamond, D. W. and Dybvig, P. H. (1983) Bank Runs, Deposit Insurance, and Liquidity, *Journal of Political Economy*, 91, 3, 401–19.

Dornbusch, R. (1991) Policies to Move from Stabilization to Growth, *Proceedings of the World Bank Annual Conference on Development Economics*, Washington, DC: The World Bank, 19–48.

Goodhart, C. A. E. (1988) *The Evolution of Central Banks*, Cambridge and London: MJT Press.

Mishkin, F. (1991) Asymmetric Information and Financial Crises: A Historical Perspective, in R. G. Hubbard (ed.), *Financial Markets and Financial Crises*, Chicago: Chicago University Press, 69–108.

Mishkin, F. S. (1996) *Understanding Financial Crises: A Developing Country Perspective*, Washington, DC: The World Bank.

Rajan, R. G. (1996) Why Banks Have a Future: Toward a New Theory of Commercial Banking, *Journal of Applied Corporate Finance*, 9, 2, Summer, 114–29.

Sargent, T. J. (1986) Reaganomics and Credibility, in Sargent, T. J. *Rational Expectations and Inflation*, New York et al.: Harper & Row.

Semenkov, V. (1999) August 98 as a Turning Point of Russian Reforms, paper presented at the Klaffenbach conference.

Stremme, M. (1998) *The Asian Virus – Financial Markets and Economic Policy in Russia*, IPC Working Paper, 19, Frankfurt.

Winkler, A. (1996) Time to Stabilise Stabilisation Policy, *Politekonom*, 2, 28–9 (in Russian).

Winkler, A. (1997) *Financial Development, Economic Growth and Corporate Governance*, Johann Wolfgang Goethe Universität, Fachbereich Wirtschaftswissenschaften, Working Paper Series: Finance, 12, Frankfurt am. Main.

III
Poland

6

Poland and International Financial Turbulences of the Second Half of the 1990s

Zbigniew Polański[1]

1 Introduction

Poland is one of the few transition countries that has been relatively unaffected by the worldwide financial turbulence of the second half of the 1990s. Obviously this was not the case for other Central-East European countries: Hungary (in 1995), the Czech Republic (in 1997) and Russia (in 1998) are prominent examples of transition economies that became victims of financial market upheavals. Thus, a question emerges: why, despite the fact that Poland's close neighbours suffered from financial turbulence, has Poland been basically immune from this turmoil? Or more provocatively: is Poland immune to financial contagion?

In what follows we will study the Polish case, making an attempt to answer these questions. We start, however, by looking at the impact of recent international turbulence on Poland to show that such impact did take place, although it was clearly much less dramatic than in the aforementioned countries. In the next section we will look at economic policies conducted by the authorities to assess the factors behind the relatively stable economic development of Poland. In the final section of the paper we will try to outline future developments asking about potential dangers. We conclude with some general remarks.

2 Developments in Poland's economic performance in the 1990s

In this section we look briefly at the main features of Poland's economic performance since the early 1990s. First, we deal with longer-term developments, then move to more recent issues.

2.1   Poland's economic development in the 1990s: A general overview

After 1989–91, when strong recession was accompanied by very high inflation,[2] Poland entered a phase of economic growth. In the two years of 1990 and 1991 its statistically recorded GDP declined by approximately 14 per cent, but in 1992 economic growth resumed. Soon after that Poland became one of the fastest growing countries in Europe. As early as 1995 its real GDP was larger than in 1989, Poland being the first among post- communist countries to surpass its pre-transformation level of income. In 1998 Poland was one of the three post-communist countries (the other two being Slovenia and Slovakia) to regain the output levels of 1989.[3] In the case of Poland GDP was approximately 22 per cent larger than in 1989.

Table 6.1 shows that strong economic growth has been accompanied by decreasing inflation. The inflation rate declined slowly over the years, but followed a consistent pattern. In October 1998 a symbolic event took place: for the first time in 18 years the yearly CPI inflation rate

Table 6.1   Poland's economic development, 1992–98

Item	1992	1993	1994	1995	1996	1997	1998
1. GDP	2.6	3.8	5.2	7.0	6.0	6.8	4.8
2. Inflation[a]	44.3	37.6	29.5	21.6	18.5	13.2	8.6
3. Investment[b]	2.3	2.9	9.2	16.9	19.7	21.7	14.5
4. Individual Consumption	2.3	5.2	4.3	3.6	8.3	6.9	4.9
5. Current Account/GDP							
5.1. On cash basis[c]	1.1	−0.7	2.4	4.6	−1.0	−3.0	−4.4
5.2. On transaction basis[d]	–	–	1.0	0.7	−2.3	−4.0	−4.4
6. Fiscal balances/GDP							
6.1. State budget[e]	−6.1	−3.1	−3.3	−3.3	−3.4	−2.6	−2.5
6.2. Public sector	−7.1	−4.5	−3.7	−3.0	−4.4	−2.6	−2.7
7. Unemployment rate	14.3	16.4	16.0	14.9	13.2	10.3	10.4

Note: Items 1–4 are percentage changes from previous year. Items 5–7 are ratios expressed in per cent.

[a]   Consumer Price Index. December to December.

[b]   Gross Fixed Capital Formation.

[c]   Current account of the annual balance of payments drawn up on the basis of payments settled and registered by Polish banks.

[d]   Current account of the annual balance of payments recording all transactions between Poland and all other countries.

[e]   Privatization proceeds excluded from budgetary revenue.

Source: Polish Central Statistical Office, National Bank of Poland and Ministry of Finance.

was at one-digit. Disinflation proved to be sustainable and in February 1999 CPI inflation was at a mere 5.6 per cent.

Since the mid-1990s these developments have been accompanied (and to some extent generated) by other phenomena registered in Table 6.1: strong investment and consumption spending, a relatively large but sustainable budget deficit,[4] and declining unemployment rate. In 1996 a growing balance of payments current account deficit appeared, raising public concern about its sustainability.[5]

In the course of our discussion we will return to the issue of the current account deficit, suggesting that neither its origins nor the way it is financed should give rise to major concern. At this point let us look at Figure 6.1 which shows that the developments visible in Table 6.1 have been accompanied by quickly growing foreign reserves since 1994. In 1998 alone NBP gross official reserves increased by 32.5 per cent.

2.2 Poland's economic developments in a world of financial turbulence: 1997–98

The information provided so far suggests long-term, sustainable, and relatively balanced economic growth. Obviously, since 1992 Poland has faced neither a reversal in economic activity nor in inflation reduction. Since the middle of the decade Poland has enjoyed a booming and relatively stable economy.

Since the December 1994 Mexican crisis, we have been witnessing a new wave of international financial upheavals. With the start of the Asian crisis in mid-1997, and the summer 1998 Russian crisis, financial turbulence has increasingly damaged the financial and real sectors of many economies. Is it possible that Poland somehow avoided the contagion effect? Let us have a closer look at the data for 1998 shown in Table 6.1 and the quarterly data provided in Table 6.2.

It can be seen from Table 6.1 that in 1998 economic growth considerably decelerated, and unemployment rate stopped its decline. Table 6.2 sheds additional light. Since mid-1997 we can observe a gradual slowdown in economic activity; as a result in the summer of 1998 GDP growth was 5 per cent. As we will see in a moment this reduction of GDP rate was partly due to internal policy measures. However, the 'exports' column in Table 6.2 suggests that the role of foreign trade in the deceleration of growth was considerable: in the first three quarters of 1998 the volume of Polish exports consistently declined. This clearly suggests that the *Polish economy was hit by the world-wide financial turbulence before the Russian crisis.*[6]

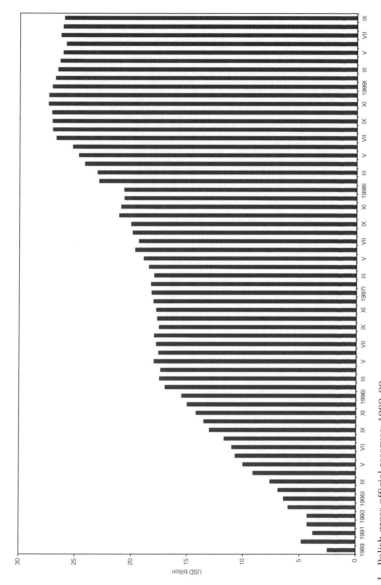

Figure 6.1 Polish gross official reserves: 1989–99
Source: National Bank of Poland.

Table 6.2 Selected indicators of Poland's economic development in 1997–98

Year and quarter	GDP[a]	Unemploy-ment rate[b]	Exports[c]	Imports[c]	Current account[d]	Months of import cover[e]
1997						
I	6.9	12.6	−1.5	−5.1	−1534	5.8
II	7.5	11.6	6.3	11.4	−1194	6.3
III	6.7	10.6	1.3	0.7	−910	6.3
IV	6.4	10.3	13.4	13.5	−674	6.1
I–IV	6.8		13.7	22.0	−4312	6.1
1998						
I	6.4	10.4	−0.4	−4.8	−1998	6.4
II	5.4	9.6	−2.3	6.8	−665	7.1
III	5.0	9.6	−2.5	1.8	−1215	7.4
IV	2.9	10.4	4.2	1.8	−2980	7.1
I–IV	4.8		9.4	14.6	−6858	7.0

Notes:
[a] Yearly changes (quarterly GDP related to the corresponding quarter of previous year).
[b] End of period. In per cent.
[c] In constant prices. Quarterly changes (except for I–IV which are year on year changes).
[d] In US$ million.
[e] NBP gross official reserves divided by the average value of one month imports of goods in the quarter (or year) in question.

Source: Polish Central Statistical Office and National Bank of Poland.

Due to the August 1998 Russian crisis, at the end of the summer the Polish current account considerably worsened. While in August the current account reached an unexpected positive balance (281 USD million), in September it became deeply negative (−1295 USD million), the last quarter exhibiting substantial increase in the size of the current account gap. The merchandise trade balance worsened as financial inflows resulting from exports declined while outflows due to imports continued to grow. Similar developments happened to the services balance. However, the Russian crisis impacted more visibly on the item 'unclassified flows balance' which mostly reflects monetary flows resulting from unregistered cross-border trade between Poland and her Eastern neighbours. By the end of 1998 the *positive* balance of these unclassified flows was by approximately half lower than in the summer months. Since September unemployment had been increasing and by the end of February 1999 its rate reached 11.9 per cent, that is, it returned to the level of mid-1997. Simultaneously, GDP growth declined to less than 3 per cent in the last quarter of 1998. From October 1998 to

February 1999 industrial production declined every month, so that in February 1999 it was lower by 5.8 per cent compared with February 1998.

The visible deceleration of economic activity suggests that the slow-down of the world economy – after a time lag – had impacted on the Polish economy. The sharp increase of the current account deficit in the course of the second half of 1998 indicate that the Polish economy had been hit by the Russian crisis. Not surprisingly the Government lowered its initial, spring 1998, budgetary forecast of GDP growth for 1999 from 6.1 per cent to 5.1 per cent in the final version of the budgetary bill submitted to the Parliament in early autumn 1998.

The last column in Table 6.2 confirms, however, the positive developments visible in Figure 6.1. During most of 1998 the monthly cover of imports by NBP reserves was increasing, which is not surprising in the situation of quickly growing foreign reserves. This behaviour of reserves and import cover, together with other data, points out, however, to an important conclusion: *the transmission of international upheavals into Poland was basically through the real sector – through foreign trade, and in particular through the decline of exports.* Indeed, the Polish central bank has not intervened *directly* on the foreign exchange market since the end of July, that is, before the Russian crisis started.[7] Even during the peak of the Russian crisis NBP reserves did not decrease.[8] As a matter of fact, from August 1998 to January 1999 Polish gross official reserves remained virtually unchanged at over 27 USD billion.[9] (As Figure 6.1 shows, in February and March 1999 we can observe some decline in the dollar value of Polish reserves which was due to the weakness of the euro and the appreciation of US dollar at that time.)[10]

The worldwide financial upheavals of the second half of the 1990s did impact on Poland's economic development but, as suggested, they were mostly transmitted through the real sector. However, *at least as yet, international turmoil has neither produced major changes nor a reversal in Poland's long-term development trends.*

3   Searching for solid fundamentals: Poland's economic policy in the 1990s

Why was Poland relatively immune from the contagion effects? In order to answer this question we will look at so-called 'fundamentals',[11] and at economic policy responses to the mounting international financial turbulence. We discuss four basic issues. First, the main changes in

Polish foreign trade patterns in the post-communist environment are considered. Second, financial system issues are briefly analysed. Third, internal macroeconomic policy developments are discussed. Fourth, international finance questions are studied.

3.1 Changes in foreign trade in the early 1990s

In order to explain the relative immunity of the Polish economy to international financial crises, and in particular to the 1998 Russian crisis, we have to go back to issues of late 1980s and early 1990s. At the beginning of this decade Poland changed its main trade partners. As a result of political and economic changes that took place in Poland in 1989–90, and the collapse of both the Soviet Union and the Council for Mutual Economic Assistance (Comecon) in 1991, the composition of Polish exports and imports became mostly oriented to the Western world. See Table 6.3.

The 1990s reorientation of Poland's trade towards the West was far reaching. In the 1996–97 period approximately two-thirds of Polish exports were directed to the EU and less than one-quarter to the post-communist European countries (Commonwealth of Independent

Table 6.3 Poland's main trading partners, 1988–96 (selected years)

Year	Share (in per cent) of main countries in total Polish: Exports		Imports	
1988	1. USSR	24.5	1. USSR	23.3
	2. West Germany	12.4	2. West Germany	13.0
	3. Czechoslovakia	6.0	3. Czechoslovakia	6.4
1991	1. Germany	29.4	1. Germany	26.5
	2. Former USSR	11.0	2. Former USSR	14.1
	3. United Kingdom	7.1	3. Austria	6.3
1994	1. Germany	35.7	1. Germany	27.4
	2. The Netherlands	5.9	2. Italy	8.4
	3. Russia	5.4	3. Russia	6.8
1996	1. Germany	34.4	1. Germany	24.7
	2. Russia	6.8	2. Italy	9.9
	3. Italy	5.3	3. Russia	6.8
	4. The Netherlands	4.8	4. United Kingdom	5.9
	5. France	4.4	5. France	5.5
	6. Ukraine	4.0	6. USA	4.4
	7. United Kingdom	3.9	7. The Netherlands	3.8
	8. The Czech Republic	3.5	8. The Czech Republic	3.1

Source: Polish Central Statistical Office.

States countries included). Of imports, over 60 per cent originated in EU countries while only approximately 15 per cent were from post-communist European countries. The collapse of exports to and the decline of imports from Russia further oriented Polish foreign trade towards the EU. In 1998 Polish exports to the EU accounted for 68.3 per cent, while imports from the EU accounted for 65.9 per cent.

The 1990s changes in the structure of Polish foreign trade flows point out, however, at the development of other channels of transmission of international economic turbulence. The new geographical diversification of Polish foreign trade means that Poland is now more exposed to economic fluctuations taking place in the West. In consequence, one has to note that in 1998 Poland was not only directly hit by the Russian crisis but that it reached her also indirectly through its impact on Poland's other main trading partners. As already suggested, in the first half of 1998 Poland's declining exports should be attributed to developments in Western Europe which echoed the 1997 Asian crisis. Furthermore, the new structure of Polish foreign trade means that EU countries' business cycle position is of key importance for Poland's economic activity. Obviously, the sharp slowdown of the EU economy, and the German economy in particular, in the last quarter of 1998, was clearly felt in Poland.

3.2   Creating a new and more efficient financial system

Similarly to other post-communist countries Poland inherited from the socialist economic period a highly underdeveloped and inefficient banking system. As in remaining post-communist countries both non-bank financial institutions and financial markets were practically non-existent.

At the end of the 1980s and in the first half of the 1990s Poland set up the legal and economic basis for a market type financial system.[12] Initially this process was accompanied by a major bad loans crisis. As can be seen from Table 6.4 this reached its zenith in 1993. At the beginning of that year, however, a special legal act designed to help solve the crisis became effective. The Law on Financial Restructuring of State Enterprises and Banks followed a *decentralized approach* to solve the crisis. Despite some direct governmental involvement, it was basically up to the banks to solve their problems with debtors. This approach was successful: banks not only cleaned out their portfolios from non-performing loans but, more importantly, in the process also learned how to evaluate credit and other types of risks. Thus, they learned how to avoid creating new bad loans.[13]

Table 6.4 Bad loans in Poland, 1992–98 (%)

Item	1992	1993	1994	1995	1996	1997	1998
1. Classified loans/GDP	6.1	6.0	5.0	3.8	2.8	2.5	2.6
2. Classified loans/total loans	30.1	31.2	28.3	21.5	13.4	10.6	10.5
3. Classified loans[a]							
3.1. Substandard	30.7	22.8	21.0	23.5	29.0	35.9	36.9
3.2. Doubtful	30.7	19.5	18.0	15.6	12.1	10.4	16.4
3.3. Lost	38.6	57.7	61.0	60.9	58.9	53.6	46.7

Notes:
[a] Figures may not add to 100.0 due to rounding.
Source: National Bank of Poland and Polish Central Statistical Office.

Table 6.4 shows the statistical aspect of this process, confirming that up to 1997 the relative volume of non-performing loans was gradually and consistently decreasing. During most of 1998 the process continued, however, by the end of the year the volume of classified loans stopped declining and by some measures even slightly increased. This was due not only to the Russian crisis. Although three major Polish banks were involved in the Russian market and, consequently, suffered from the turbulence and the following decline of trade, some rise of bad loans was also due to internal developments.[14]

In the first half of the 1990s Poland adopted the essential part of EU bank regulations and other prudential norms worked out by the international community. At the Central Bank an efficient supervision department (The General Inspectorate of Banking Supervision) was created. In the mid-1990s the Bank Guarantee Fund started operating. In 1997–98 Central Bank autonomy was further increased by the new Constitution of the Republic of Poland and the new National Bank of Poland Act, so that now the Central Bank is fully committed to both monetary and financial stability.

There is an ongoing process of bank modernization, consolidation and privatization in Poland. Since the Polish economy is lacking, among other things, capital to finance this process, the role of foreign investors in the banking system has been systematically increasing. *By the end of 1998 half of Poland's banking system was owned by foreigners* (see Table 6.5).[15]

The Polish financial system is essentially a bank-oriented one. Thus, other financial institutions and the capital market play a less important role. This is particularly true in the case of the stock exchange. Trading on the Warsaw Stock Exchange (WSE) began in April 1991. By and large

Table 6.5 Foreign investments in Polish banking sector by countries at the end of 1998 (%)

Country	of total bank capital	of total foreign capital
All countries	49.7	100.0
Main countries:		
1. Germany	15.9	32.0
2. USA	14.3	28.9
3. The Netherlands	7.0	14.0
4. France	4.5	9.1
5. Austria	3.6	7.2
6. South Korea	0.8	1.7
7. Ireland	0.8	1.6

Source: National Bank of Poland.

WSE is considered as the best regulated (in terms of transparency) and the safest among exchanges in Central and Eastern Europe.[16] However, its macroeconomic role is still very limited. In 1998 WSE capitalization was equivalent to approximately 13.5 per cent of GDP. By any standard this is not a high ratio. Furthermore, most of the equities traded, in the process of privatization generated proceeds to the state budget and not to issuing companies. Up to now the main investor on the WSE is the government.

Obviously, the Polish financial system cannot be considered as either developed or efficient. Financial deepening and monetization indicators for Poland are usually lower than for many other Central European economies. Most Polish companies rely on retained earnings to finance their development and they do not seek actively financial intermediation services. Having said all that, one must stress that in the ten years of transition, Poland managed to modernize and strengthen her financial system. This fact, together with further analysed macroeconomic issues, explains why, in Poland, the international turbulence did not turn into a financial and economic crisis.

3.3 Macroeconomic stringency

With the start of the so-called Balcerowicz plan in January 1990, Poland has not only begun an accelerated transition to a market economy but also moved into an era of tight macroeconomic policies. Of course, the degree of their restrictiveness as well as the composition of the policy mix changed over time. While the Central Bank's policy consistently focused on monetary and inflation control,[17] budget deficits fluctuated considerably in the first half of the decade (see Table 6.1).

Table 6.1 also shows that since the middle of the decade substantial government deficits were accompanied by a strong growth in investment spending and – since 1996 – by a growing current account deficit. Under these circumstances the latter was interpreted as resulting from an investment–saving imbalance. It was argued that Poland faced a kind of twin-deficit problem: the supply of savings was falling short in the face of budget deficits and quickly growing investment spending. It was estimated that in 1996 the gap between domestic saving as a percentage of GDP and total investment as a percentage of GDP was approximately 3 percentage points.[18] The economy needed injections of external capital to continue its quick development. Consequently, Poland faced a capital inflow which pushed the balance of payments current account into deficit.

Although from a historical perspective it can be easily argued that in 1996 the situation was fully under control (see Table 6.6), in December that year the Polish Central Bank decided to increase, through open market operations, the interbank market rate, beginning a policy aimed at 'cooling down' the economy. Such a move seemed justified as fiscal deficits in 1996 showed a tendency to increase (see Table 6.1) and bank credit supply was quickly expanding. In 1996 alone, total bank loans increased by more than 40 per cent; consumer credits more than doubled.

Taking advantage of its decision-making autonomy the National Bank of Poland (NBP) continued to tighten its policy in the course of 1997. As inflation was still high, the current account gap was widening, strong credit expansion continued, heavy pressures to expand the budget deficit were taking place (1997 was an election year and in the summer floods in South-West Poland additionally motivated the Parliament to increase budget expenditure), and the Czech currency crisis and

Table 6.6 Selected Polish external financial safety indicators in 1996–98 (%)

Indicators	1996	1997	1998
1. Foreign direct investments/Current account deficit[a]	202.7	70.8	72.4
2. Foreign debt service/Exports	8.6	6.7	10.9

Notes:
[a] On cash basis (see note 5).

Source: National Bank of Poland.

South-East Asian crisis developed, the NBP decided that its policies should be fully committed to economic stability. In the next subsection we will describe NBP policy initiatives in the area of international finance. Here we will concentrate briefly on internal economic policy responses.

In the first half of 1997 NBP increased twice – the already very high – banks' non-remunerated obligatory reserve requirements. As a result in 1997 (and in 1998) the average ratio of these reserves to banks' deposit base was close to 12 per cent. In the face of Parliament's decision to increase budgetary expenditures to finance the reconstruction of the areas hit by the 1997 summer floods, the NBP decided to increase its basic (administrative) rates by 2 to 2.5 per cent in early August. These decisions, however, did not curb credit expansion enough. Consequently, the NBP took an unprecedented action: from mid-September until mid-December 1997 it collected (at a rate slightly above market rate) 6– and 9–month deposits directly from the public. Only after this NBP move did banks reduce the pace of lending. However, despite the fact that real deposit and credits rates were 5 percentage points higher by end of the year than at its beginning, overall in 1997 bank lending increased by more than 30 per cent.

In 1998 NBP did not increase the interest rates. As the inflation rate declined, in the first half of the year real rates (measured ex-post) reached approximately 10 per cent. At this time banks reduced the rate of credit expansion. More importantly, the new government, empowered after the September 1997 elections, started a tighter fiscal policy, among other things refusing, from the beginning of 1998 to finance budgetary deficits through Central Bank credit.[19]

The 1998 developments permitted a change in the policy mix. From spring 1998 nominal interest rates were gradually lowered, but as a result of an unexpected decline in inflation rates, real interest rates remained at the 10 per cent level. It was not until the end of 1998 and the beginning of 1999 that real rates declined, reaching approximately 7 to 8 per cent.

The 1997–98 restrictive policy helped to avoid the destabilization of the economy. This would undoubtedly have taken place if these rapid, and sometimes controversial, policy measures had not been introduced. For most of 1998 the current account deficit was under control – it only increased more than expected after the Russian crisis impacted on foreign trade flows (from September 1998). In this sense it can be argued that the policies described above helped to avoid a traditional (i.e., through a currency crisis) 'import' of international turmoil. Obviously

Polish authorities had correctly anticipated possible developments and took proper actions in due time.

Two observations, however, must be made. First, the policy of 'cooling down' proved to be costly. Probably the 1997–98 slowdown of Polish economy can to some extent be attributed to this policy. Also the very small decline in non-performing loans, signaled in the previous subsection, can be linked to the policy of high interest rates.[20] Second, the above outline of the 1997–98 policies is incomplete as it is basically restricted to domestic issues. Next we briefly present international aspects of Polish policy responses to the mounting worldwide financial turbulence in the second half of the 1990s.

3.4 International aspects of Polish macroeconomic policy

Since 1995 the evolution of the Polish exchange rate regime has mainly resulted from international developments.[21] Changes in the exchange rate system have reflected authorities' responses to problems posed by the very fact that Poland in the course of the first half of the 1990s evolved into a typical small open economy subject to the logic of the interest rate parity condition.

The 1994–95 Mexican crisis triggered changes aiming at greater exchange rate flexibility. Until May 1995 Poland had a pre-announced crawling-peg exchange rate regime.[22] This system, together with high interest rates resulting from the policies aimed at reducing inflation, in the context of sharply improving economic situation (see Table 6.1) and the search for new opportunities by investors who withdrew from Mexico, led to a considerable, and unexpected, inflow of foreign capital. At this time Poland enjoyed a current account surplus, which – together with the inflow of foreign direct investments (FDIs) and portfolio capital – led to a quick increase of NBP's foreign reserves. In 1995 alone they increased 2.5 times (see Figure 6.1). Consequently, it was considered that the exchange rate system ought to be less rigid and more exchange rate risk should be introduced into foreign investors' calculations.

In mid-May 1995 Poland introduced a *crawling band exchange rate regime*. The zloty was allowed to fluctuate in a band of +/ − 7 per cent from a central parity rate which was subject to a crawling devaluation. Figure 6.2 shows exchange rate developments under this system. As a matter of clarification it has to be added that in the Figure only an approximation to the market rate is given through the so-called fixing rate, that is, a weighted average of five currencies[23] at a rate which was fixed daily (on the basis of market conditions) by the Central Bank.

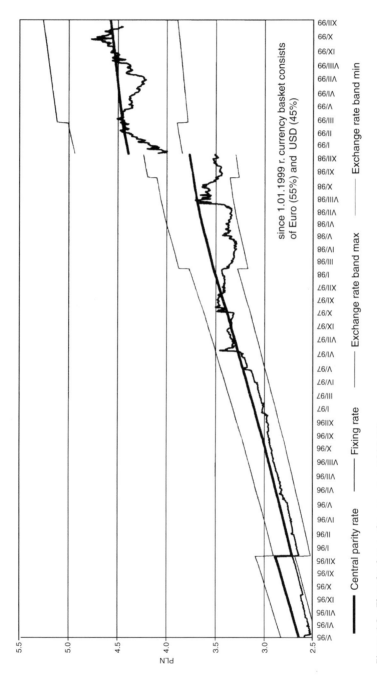

Figure 6.2 Zloty basket exchange rates, 1995–99
Source: National Bank of Poland.

Figure 6.2 clearly shows that the zloty's exchange rate acted as a shock absorber, in other words, currency flexibility proved to be a buffer against shocks taking place in the international environment. As shown, usually the market ('fixing') rate was below the central parity rate meaning pressure for the appreciation of the zloty. It is easy to notice that (with the exception of the summer of 1997)[24] the zloty displayed a tendency to devalue only when international financial turmoil was taking place, for example, during the currency crisis in the Czech Republic (May 1997), during the South-East Asian crisis (autumn 1997) and at the time of the Russian crisis (August–September 1998). Figure 6.2 confirms that a flexible exchange rate shields the domestic economy from external turbulence. This also explains our earlier observation that international upheavals were not transmitted into Poland through the financial sphere but rather through real flows.[25]

In 1998 (and in the first months of 1999) the crawling-band system was subject to important changes. Before we elaborate on them, however, other developments must be stressed. In the first half of the 1990s the scope of convertibility of the Polish zloty was gradually increased, covering all current account transaction and most capital account transactions. This was recognized internationally: in mid-1995 Poland officially complied with the International Monetary Fund Article VIII standard of convertibility.[26] In November 1996 Poland joined the Organization for Economic Cooperation and Development (OECD) and committed herself to make gradual changes in her foreign exchange law aiming at further opening of the capital account, so that by the year 2000 Poland could enjoy full convertibility of her currency.[27]

The other development taking place in the second half of the 1990s which must be strongly stressed, is that the volume of capital inflows into Poland considerably increased. Although on the per capita basis many other post-communist countries, most notably Hungary and the Czech Republic, benefited much more from foreign capital inflows than Poland, it is also true that in absolute terms it was Poland which benefited most from these inflows. It was estimated that between 1990 and 1998 over 30 USD billion of foreign direct investments flew into Poland.[28] What is more, this inflows follow an increasing pattern: 1998 was the top year with an inflow of FDIs of approximately 10 USD billion. It is increasingly probable that the Russian crisis did not have a negative impact on FDIs flowing into Poland; actually, it seems that Poland may benefited from the fact that some investors changed their mind and moved their investments from Russia to Poland.

As shown in Table 6.6, the current account deficit has been mostly financed by foreign direct investments. Thus, *the structure of capital flowing into Poland makes it fully sustainable*. This structure of capital inflows is due to several factors. On the one hand, it results from the size of the Polish goods market and the underdevelopment of the capital market. On the other hand, however, one should stress the role of the flexible exchange rate in discouraging speculative investors.

In the face of the growing openness of the Polish capital account, and aiming to improve the control of money supply and at achieving more efficient anti-inflation policy, the Monetary Policy Committee (MPC) of the National Bank of Poland[29] widened the fluctuation band and reduced the rate of depreciation. The MPC in several moves widened the exchange rate band from $+/-7$ per cent to $+/-12.5$ per cent and reduced the monthly rate of crawl from 1 per cent to 0.5 per cent in 1998. In March 1999 the band was further widened to $+/-15$ per cent and the rate of crawl was reduced to 0.3 per cent (see Figure 6.2).

As mentioned earlier, at the same time interest rates were lowered several times, further reducing interest rate differentials between the Polish and international financial markets, thus, diminishing incentives for short-term investment in Poland. Indeed, because of its good overall situation Poland could afford to cut interest rates during the peak of the Russian crisis: on 10 September 1998 the MPC unexpectedly lowered the NBP intervention rate[30] from 19 to 18 per cent without any negative impact on the volume of capital flowing into Poland. As also mentioned earlier, since the end of July 1998 the NBP has stopped actively intervening in the foreign exchange market.

Polish fundamentals are clearly not perfect, but it has to be stressed that *most of them have improved over the course of the decade*. Obviously, the growing negative current account can create concern. Usually, a current account gap of 5 per cent of GDP is considered dangerous. However, the way the current account deficit is financed in Poland strongly suggests that it is sustainable.

4   What lies ahead?

So far the analysis and description has concentrated mostly on macroeconomic fundamentals. Thus, if we consider the theories of financial crises, it means that we referred to so-called 'first generation crises'. These crises are basically predictable and it explains our generally positive outlook concerning the low probability of a currency attack in Poland.

However, it is often argued that in the 1990s we mostly observe 'second generation crises' which are basically unpredictable.[31] Therefore, a crucial question emerges concerning the possibility of such a crisis in Poland.

Although the answer to this question is of key importance, it is not clear what are the direct causes triggering a second generation type of a financial crisis. Nonetheless, it is obvious that some general conditions must be fulfilled for a self-fulfilling currency attack to occur, even if historically in most cases the direct factors triggering the crises were different.

The economic literature suggests two such general conditions. First, capital liberalization, especially in the area of highly mobile, short-term capital. Second, there must be some weakness 'which will prevent the authorities from conducting a full-fledged defense of its currency by raising the interest rate',[32] for example, a weak banking system or the budgetary costs of such a decision.

Taking into account these two general factors it can be pointed out that Poland proved to be basically immune to the 1990s international financial turbulence exactly because these two reasons were not fulfilled. On the one hand, both the convertibility of the zloty has been only gradually expanded and the structure of capital inflows has been dominated by FDIs, thus reducing decisively the mobility of capital flows. On the other hand, as stressed, economic policy in Poland in the entire 1990s was geared towards solid fundamentals. Thus, until now Poland has fulfilled neither the conditions necessary for the first type of crisis nor the second type of crisis.

There is always, however, a possibility that things may change. This is particularly true in a transition country like Poland, aiming for a quick accession to EU and later on to EMU. The fast transformation of social, political and economic institutions increases dangers, which might be conducive to capital inflows reversals.

In 1999 Poland started to implement four important reforms. All of them are related to the public sector, but have direct implications both for the development of financial markets and the fiscal position of the government. In particular, pension reform (a switch from the pay-as-you-go system to a mixed system in which part of employees' contributions is invested through pension funds on the capital market) is a costly one for the state budget, and it should contribute to the development of the capital market.[33] Although in the long-run (given the demographic processes) such a reform is indispensable, in the short run it is creating tensions in the state budget. There is also a potential danger that a quick development of investment activities can result in an overheating stock market.

In such circumstances macroeconomic policy should be rather restrictive, which is not easy given the current problems with economic slowdown and the arising tensions in the state budget. Taking into account the latter, monetary policy should maintain the tight stance.

In September 1998 NBP's Monetary Policy Committee published a document entitled *Medium-Term Strategy of Monetary Policy (1999–2003)* which outlines a scenario for monetary policy up to 2003 – to the moment when Poland should be ready to join European Union. The basic goal of the *Strategy* is to reduce the inflation rate below 4 per cent by the year 2003.

The document assumes that Poland will move towards a floating exchange rate regime before joining the EU and entering the ERM 2 system. Our analysis of the crawling-band during 1995–98 suggests that a floating rate is a useful tool to discourage short-term capital inflows. Thus, a freely floating exchange rate should protect the internal markets from speculative capital movements. As Poland, despite the existing budgetary tensions, seems to fulfill the conditions for a smooth intro-duction of a floating exchange rate system, it should be expected that a final step to this regime will be made rather soon.[34]

However, a key question in this context is whether a floating exchange rate is a sufficient tool to fully protect the economy from unwanted capital movements. The orthodox approach to this problem is that a pure float is sufficient. Such an approach, however, does not encompass all the intricacies of an emerging, post-communist economy. First, it cannot be assumed that Poland will have an unconditional free float exchange rate mechanism as countries rather try to influence their exchange rates, even when they officially follow flexible policies.[35] Sec-ond, Poland has small financial markets, particularly the foreign exchange market, which would be very easy to destabilize. Third, Poland, in common with other post-communist countries, faces an appreciation of the equilibrium real exchange rate.[36] This, together with the two previously mentioned factors, and possible dangers result-ing from fast institutional changes, may lead to unwanted capital inflows followed by their sudden reversals, deeply destabilizing the exchange rate and damaging the real economy in the process.

Consequently, we make a point that despite commitments made to the international community Poland should retain controls of short-term capital flows in the years to come. Two issues, however, must be made clear. Such capital controls should be only an additional, temporary instrument for policymakers, the main role being played by a tight macroeconomic policy and a flexible exchange rate. Second, capital controls do not have to be only of administrative nature. The well known Chilean experience with mandatory, non-yielding deposits taxing short-term capital inflows ought to be seriously considered.[37]

5   Conclusions

In this chapter we have shown that there is nothing particularly surprising in the fact that Poland has been relatively unaffected by the international turmoil of the last few years. Poland, a typical small open economy now, is obviously not immune to world-wide developments. However, proper macroeconomic and institutional policies have substantially reduced their negative impact.

As we have demonstrated Poland's good performance should not be attributed to only one factor, but to a group of factors resulting from strategic choices. The gradual and consistent Polish economic policies of the 1990s, which emphasized a need for solid fundamentals (both macroeconomic and institutional), are the main reason behind the fact that Poland has been relatively successful in a world dominated by financial contagion effects.

International economic and financial turmoil has been basically transmitted into Poland through trade links. Although the 1998 Russian crisis had an impact, developments in the EU, have shown to be of crucial importance for Poland. Unless there is a severe worldwide recession, Poland's 1990s long-term development trends should not be reversed. International turmoil may, however, result in a further economic slowdown.

Notes

1   Warsaw School of Economics (Chair of Monetary Policy) and National Bank of Poland (Research Department). The views presented here are those of the author and do not necessarily reflect the position of the NBP. I express my gratitude to M. Golajewska, P. Sotomska-Krzysztofik, and P. Wyczański, all from NBP, for providing statistical data, graphs and other information.

   The initial version of the chapter was presented at the conference 'Financial turbulence and capital markets in transition countries' organized by Chemnitz University of Technology (4–5 February 1999). Let me thank the participants of the conference, and in particular the discussants, for all comments.

2   See for instance Polański (1992, 1993 and 1995). A short outline of Polish inflation in 1989–95 can be found in Pujol and Griffiths (1998).

3   European Bank for Reconstruction and Development (quoted from *The Economist* 5–11 December 1998, p. 138).

4   It should be noted that the primary balance (i.e., excluding interest payments) of the Polish state budget has been positive since 1993.

5   In Table 6.1 we present two measures of Polish current account deficit. Balance of payments data based on cash basis are published every month and, consequently, are used for current decision making. However, these data relate only to payments registered by the Polish banking system. On the other hand, balance of payments based on transaction basis covers all transactions (thus, this is a 'true' balance of payments), but in Poland it is compiled only once a year.

6   Gomulka (1999) argues that the export performance of the second quarter of 1998 was due to developments in Western Europe and developing countries which in turn echoed the South-East Asian crisis of autumn 1997.

7   It has to be added here that in 1998 all *direct* NBP interventions were aimed at reducing the upward pressure on the zloty and not at reducing the downward pressure. To complete the picture it should be added, however, that up to early June 1999 every business day NBP conducted so called 'fixing transactions'. That is, banks were allowed to submit bids to the Central Bank concerning foreign exchange transactions. Among others, these bids were used to calculate the Central Bank foreign exchange rate. From June 1999 such fixing transactions were abolished which is equivalent to say that from that moment NBP stopped also intervening *indirectly* on the foreign exchange market.

8   However, one has to mention that during the very peak of the Russian crisis there was a capital flight from Poland of approximately 800 USD million in short-term investment which reduced commercial banks' reserves.

9   Despite the fact that in December Poland unexpectedly bought part of its outstanding foreign debt (Brady bonds of 727.8 USD million).

10 Additionally, the last day of March 1999 Poland, as scheduled, repaid part of its debt to Paris Club banks (institutions whose loans have been guaranteed by governments). Before that NBP gross official reserves reached 27 USD billion again.

11 When speaking about incorrect fundamentals we usually refer to certain macroeconomic variables (or their ratios) which underlie financial crises (more precisely, so-called 'first generation crises'; we will return to this point in section 4). Traditionally, the most often quoted fundamentals are inflation, credit growth, budgetary (public sector) balance, current account deficit and the stock of foreign exchange reserves. It should be noted that in this section we stress one variable, which is not considered to be a typical fundamental – the condition of the financial system. Therefore, when we speak about Polish fundamentals we do not only refer to macroeconomic variables, but also to fundamentals of an institutional nature, which is not surprising in a country building its market institutions practically from scratch.

12 For more details see Wyczañski (1993) and Polañski (1997).

13 For details see Polañski (1995). For a more recent assessment of the Polish approach to bank restructuring *vis-à-vis* other post-communist European countries see Borish and Montes-Negret (1998).

14 Two of them should be mentioned. First, problems with the repayment of consumer credit resulting from the tightening of monetary policy in 1997–98 (see next subsection). Second, changes in the classification of credits in the portfolio of the largest Polish bank (The State Savings Bank) aimed at cleaning it from credits granted to finance home construction in communist times.

15 Two issues, however, should be made clear. First, data in Table 6.5 refer to total foreign capital involvement in the Polish banking system, i.e., it does include minority ownership stakes. Consequently, the actual control of banks by foreign investors is lower than the Table suggests. Second, foreign banks are only beginning to expand deposit and credit activities in Poland. Thus, their role on the deposit and credit markets is much lower than their participation in total bank capital.

16 See for instance *The Economist* (1996).

17 A short description of Polish monetary policy from 1990 until 1997 can be found in Polański (1998).

18 Orlowski (1999).

19 Actually, financing budgetary deficits by NBP is explicitly forbidden by the 1997 Polish Constitution. The merit of the government is that it stopped using this way of financing deficits before the law required it.

20 As is well known high interest rates provide additional incentives for the adverse selection problems. It is very likely that consumer credit problems in 1998 (see note 14) originated to some degree from tight monetary control.

21 This was not the case in the first half of the decade. Until 1994 Polish exchange rate developments were subject to both anti-inflationary policy considerations and Polish exporters' price competitiveness position. For more see Polański (1999).

22 The history of Polish (as well as of other selected Central and Eastern European countries) exchange rate regimes in the first half of the decade is described in detail by Radzyner and Riesinger (1996).

23 These currencies formed a basket which served (from 1991 until 1998) to peg the zloty (more exactly – to calculate its central parity rates). They were (the respective percentage weights are given in parentheses): US Dollar (45), Deutsche Mark (35), British Pound (10), French Frank (5) and Swiss Frank (5). From 1 January 1999 the basket consists of two currencies: Euro and the US Dollar (55 and 45 per cent, respectively).

24 As mentioned in subsection 3.3. at this time Poland faced heavy floods and the Parliamentary election campaign was under way.

25 A good description of the initial impact of the Russian crisis on Polish financial markets can be found in Krzak (1998).

26 According to this standard the exchange system must be free of restrictions on the making of payments and transfers for current international transactions.

27 Details can be found in OECD (1997, pp. 135–45).

28 This data is quoted from the Polish Agency for Foreign Investment. According to these statistics the largest invested amounts came from (in order of importance): Germany, USA, France, Italy, United Kingdom and the Netherlands.

29 The 1997 Polish Constitution and the NBP Act established a new NBP decision-making body, the Monetary Policy Council, in order to depoliticize monetary policy management.

30   That is, the rate used by NBP when conducting open-market operations (technically speaking, the interest rate on the 28–day NBP bill).
31   See for instance Wyplosz (1998).
32   Wyplosz (1998, pp. 4 and 15).
33   The other reforms deal with the health care service, educational system and administrative decentralization.
34   On the conditions (and experience) in moving to greater exchange rate flexibility see Eichengreen (1999).
35   In fact, in the *Strategy* it is stated that 'the NBP will maintain the right to intervene in foreign exchange markets when it recognizes a need to do so for monetary policy reasons' (NBP, 1998, p. 15).
36   For more see Halpern and Wyplosz (1996, 1998).
37   International experience concerning capital liberalization is analysed in detail by Williamson and Mahar (1998).

References

Borish, M. and Montes-Negret, F. (1998) Restructuring Distressed Banks in Transition Economies: Lessons from Central Europe and Ukraine, in G. Caprio Jr, W. C. Hunter, G. G. Kaufman and D. M. Leipziger (eds), *Preventing Bank Crises. Lessons from Recent Global Bank Failures*, Washington, DC: The World Bank.

The Economist (1996) Financial Reform in Central Europe. Time to Take Stock, 13 April, 88–9.

Eichengreen, B. (1999) Kicking the Habit: Moving from Pegged Rates to Greater Exchange Rate Flexibility, *The Economic Journal*, 109, March, C1–C14.

Gomulka, S. (1999) Szoki zewnetrzne czy bledy wlasne (External shocks or our own mistakes), *Rzeczpospolita*, 3 March.

Halpern, L. and Wyplosz, C. (1996) *Equilibrium Exchange Rate in Transition Econo-mies*, IMF Working Paper, Washington, DC, November.

Halpern, L. and Wyplosz, C. (1998), Equilibrium Exchange Rate in Transition Economies: Further Results, paper presented at Centre for Economic Policy Research/EastWest Institute Economic Policy Initiative Forum, Brussels, 20–22 November.

Krzak, M. (1998) Contagion Effects of the Russian Crisis on Central and Eastern Europe: The Case of Poland, *Focus on Transition,* Oesterreichische Nationalbank, 2.

National Bank of Poland, various publications.

NBP (1998) National Bank of Poland – Monetary Policy Council, *Medium-Term Strategy of Monetary Policy (1999–2003)*, Warsaw, September.

OECD (1997) *Code of Liberalisation of Capital Movements*, Paris: OECD.

Orlowski, W. M. (1999) Makroekonomiczne przyczyny deficytów obrotów biezacych (Macroeconomic causes of current account deficits), *Ekonomista*, 1–2, 15–30.

Polañski, Z. (1992) The Financial System in Post-Communist Countries: The Polish Lessons, *Intereconomics*, November/December, 261–268.

Polañski, Z. (1993) Wechselkurspolitik und auenwirtschaftliche Strategie im Tranformationsprozeß: das Beispiel Polen, in H. Herr and A. Westphal (eds),

Transformation in Mittel- und Osteuropa, Frankfurt/New York: Campus Verlag, 301–323.

Polañski, Z. (1995) Building a Monetary Economy in Poland, in J. Hölscher, A. Jacobsen, H. Tomann and H. Weisfeld (eds), *Bedingungen ökonomischer Entwicklung in Zentralosteuropa (Conditions of Economic Development in Central and Eastern Europe), Field Studies on Transition,* Marburg: Metropolis-Verlag, 109–153.

Polañski, Z. (1997) Polish Financial System in the 1990s, in S. Raczkowski (ed.), *Economic Transition in China and the Eastern European Countries,* Warsaw: Polish Academy of Sciences/Chinese Academy of Social Sciences, 64–78.

Polañski, Z. (1998) Polish Monetary Policy in the 1990s: A Bird's Eye View, in K. S. Vorst and W. Wemeyer (eds), *Financial Market Restructuring in Selected Central European Countries,* Aldershot: Ashgate, 7–22.

Polañski, Z. (1999), Polityka kursu walutowego w Polsce lat 90. Stabilizacja, konkurencyjnosc i przeplywy kapitalowe (Exchange rate policy in Poland in the 1990s: Stabilization, competitiveness and capital flows), *Ekonomista,* 1–2, 135–154.

Polish Central Statistical Office, various publications.

Pujol, T. and Griffiths, M. (1998) Moderate Inflation in Poland: A Real Story, in C. Cottarelli and G. Szapáry (eds), *Moderate Inflation. The Experience of Transition Economies,* Washington, DC: International Monetary Fund, National Bank of Hungary.

Radzyner, O. and Riesinger, S. (1996) Exchange Rate Policy in Transition – Developments and Challenges in Central and Eastern Europe, *Focus on Transition,* Oesterreichische Nationalbank, 1.

Williamson, J. and Mahar, M. (1998) *A Survey of Financial Liberalization,* Princeton: Princeton University.

Wyczañski, P. (1993) *Polish Banking System 1990–92,* Warsaw: Friedrich Ebert Stiftung.

Wyplosz, C. (1998) Speculative Attacks and Capital Mobility, paper presented at Centre for Economic Policy Research/EastWest Institute Economic Policy Initiative Forum, Brussels, 20–22 November.

7
Immune to Contagion or Favourable Events? Comment on Zbigniew Polañski

Alexander Karmann

Is an economy immune against financial contagion, or what are the conditions necessary for a crisis, and how does this relate to the country under consideration, in this case Poland? Polañski's chapter 'Poland and International Financial Turbulance of the Second Half of the 1990s' centres on this issue, the question of why Poland was relatively unaffected in the 1997–98 international turmoil. My commentary is split into four statements on Polañski's analysis providing a slightly modified interpretation.

1 Are there leading indicators of event risk?

The arguments cited in section 4 that the event 'financial crises' became 'unpredictable' in the late nineties are – in part – questionable: the Thai event had been produced by a decreasing credibility of the announced Baht–Dollar exchange rate peg in the presence of diminishing foreign reserves in relation to foreign financial claims (see the corresponding papers in Menkhoff, L. and B. Reszat (1998)). The Russian event was originated by deteriorating financial fundamentals (see the corresponding chapters in this volume).

In other words, the relative amount of foreign reserves seems to play a major role in an immunization strategy. Consequently, indicators characterizing sovereign risk should deserve more attention and a closer analysis. Polañski's 'months of import cover' (Table 2.6 and Fig. 6.1) is a good step into this direction but should be redefined to account for 'foreign debt payments' (to be made in the current period). Moreover, as the likelihood of a default or a moratorium is also influenced by the amount of exports, a sovereign risk indicator should also reflect the expectations about export activities, a variable which is typically quite volatile (cf. Table 6.2). Such an approach is taken in Karmann and Plate (1999).

2   What explains Poland's immunization?

Polański takes a multifactor approach to explain the relatively stable growth path of the Polish economy, especially during the Russian crisis:

- The distribution of Polish export flows has changed considerably since the late 1980's in favour of its western neighbours.
- The worldwide economic slowdown that followed the Asian crisis and the 'cooling down' policy of the National Bank of Poland (NBP), both seem to have served as – unintentional but well functioning – buffers absorbing financial turbulences.
- Monetary policy was committed to stability and directed towards appropriate capital inflows. But, increasing CB interest rates finally led to economic stagnation in 1997–98 and – as we observe in the first quarter of 1999 – lowering interest rates devaluated the zloty quite considerably. Hence, one may argue that Poland's timely immunization strategy against international financial rumour was undergone at the cost of an economic stagnation coming up periods later.
- The Polish financial system developed gradually and slowly compared to the Czech and Hungarian counterparts. It can hardly be thought of as an efficient evaluation of a modern banking system (cross-national comparisons are given in Buch (1996) and Borrish, Ding and Noel (1997)). But, we have to concede that the 'decentralization policy' of the National Bank of Poland, i.e. forcing the banks to solve their bad loan problems by themselves, dampened the moral-hazard behaviour to abuse capital infusion. Such abuses of capital inflows from monetary or governmental institutions have been observed in the Bulgarian case before 1996. Paradoxically, the slow development of the financial service industry forced foreign investors to engage mainly in FDI activities due to a lack of alternatives. This created a structure of foreign capital claims of considerably constrained mobility, thus supporting stability of the domestic financial system.

3   Are gradualism and control a good policy method?

The danger of fast transformation processes is obvious. The number of burst bubbles in emerging stock markets are prominent examples of unexpected reversals. Similarly, the immediate transition to a full floating exchange rate regime may involve high risk, especially in the case of shallow financial markets. These arguments motivate, to some extent, Polañski's preferences for temporary capital control. The new currency regulation that was introduced in Poland in January 1999 could be seen as an attempt for a financial control mechanism. Under the regulation foreigners are obliged, before implementation, to report all transfers of income payments to be taxed domestically. According to the respective public discussion, such regulatory policy will, however, result in high transaction costs foreign economic agents have to bear even in times when financial turbulences are absent. This illustrates that such limitations may considerably harm the process of foreign investment activities.

4   Concluding remarks

In conclusion, I would like to slightly modify the interpretation of Poland's 'immunization' as presented by Polañski. First, the surprisingly stable exchange rate path in the late 1990's may result from a combination of a well-designed monetary policy and the presence of some favourable events. Moreover, the stable export/import pattern between Poland and the EU countries, summing up to over two-thirds in volume, seems to give additional support for an 'immune' exchange rate path during the past years. Second, whether the Polish economy is, in general, more immune than its neighbour countries is not clear. When institutional factors play a determining role for stable economic growth of transition economies, other neighbouring countries like Hungary, having a well developed constitutional system (as pointed out by Laszlo Solyom (1999), president of the Hungarian Constitutional Court), should have been as immune as Poland.

Third, at least the 'efficiency' argument (concerning the financial system) is open to question. Maybe, and paradoxically, the non-transformation (or slow transformation) process of the financial institutions prevented Poland from suffering more from international financial waves during the Russian crisis. This view would also express some doubts about whether the Big-Bang solution is an appropriate way for transition economies to adapt their financial sector.

In the discussion on appropriate monetary policies for transition economies, some proponents suggest implementation of newer policy strategies such as inflation targeting or central bank contracting which are, in general, applicable when dealing with the problem of an inflation bias (see, for example, Karmann (1998) for a more elaborate analysis of the topic). Often, these advocates forget about the prerequisites necessary when dealing with strategies that primarily focus on inflation as a target or a benchmark for remuneration. First, the commodity bundle underlying the price level to be calculated has to be composed of only such goods and services for which market prices are available. Such data may be difficult to obtain in the case of transition economies. Even for Germany, the amount of consumption goods with (directly or indirectly) governmentally administered prices is estimated as 41.7 per cent (Sachverständigenrat 1996). Moreover, there may be quite diverging price paths for goods, typically following a flatter growth path, and for services, typically highly inflated in deregulation periods. Furthermore, the emphasis on an inflation target may become doubtful in high-inflation regimes allowing inflation to persist for a long period of time. Finally, measuring actual inflation in transition economies requires a corresponding well-developed national statistics and accounting system in order to overcome the known problems in the presence of a mixed economy consisting of official, barter and black-market activities. Having these objections in mind, we can conclude that in the context of transition economies, due to the problem of measuring inflation in transition periods, 'traditional' monetary strategies, such as NBP's gradual liberalization from a crawling band to a floating exchange rate regime, seem to be more appropriate than any other strategy that would be based directly on inflation considerations.

References

Borrish, S., Ding, W. and Noel, M. (1997) The Evolution of the State-owned Banking Sector during Transition in Central Europe, *Europe-Asia Studies*, 29, 1187–208.

Buch, C. (1996) *Creating Efficient Banking System: Theory and Evidence from Eastern Europe*, Tübingen: Mohr.

Karmann, A. (1998) Monetary Policy Strategies: From Rules to Central Bank Contracts under Contingent Target Agreements, in H. Wagner (ed.), *Current Issues in Monetary Economies*, Heidelberg, New York: Physica, 93–108.

Karmann, A. and Plate, M. M. (1999) Country-Risk Indicator. An Option Based Evaluation, to appear in G. Bol, G. Nakhaeizadeh and K.-H. Vollmer (eds), *Data Mining and Computational Finance*, Heidelberg and New York: Physica.

Menkhoff, L. and Reszat, B. (eds) (1998) *Asian Financial Markets*, Baden-Baden: Nomos.

Sachverständigenrat zur Begutachtung der gesamtwirtschaftlichen Begutachtung (1994) Den Aufschwung sichern – Arbeitsplätze schaffen, *Jahresgutachten 1994/95*, Stuttgart: Metzler-Poeschel.

Solyom, L. and Brunner, G. (1999) *Constitutional Judiciary in a New Democracy: The Hungarian Constitutional Court*, Michigan: University of Michigan Press.

IV

Czech Republic

8
Privatization and Transparency: Evidence from the Czech Republic[1]

František Turnovec

Introduction

The chapter provides a short overview of the results and implications of mass privatization in the Czech Republic and reflection on the post-privatization depression of the Czech economy. A concept of transparency of an ownership structure is addressed. A simple algebraic model of transparency of a property distribution is applied to an analysis of the ownership structure in the Czech banking sector.

1   Mass privatization in the Czech Republic

For several years Czech privatization was considered a success story. Even compared to other former communist countries the Czech Republic was exceptional in etatization with only 4 per cent of GDP produced by private sector (and 10 per cent produced by the co-operative sector) in 1989. The issue of privatization became a first priority agenda immediately after the fall of communist regime. By 1998 the private sector contribution to GDP was officially estimated to be 90 per cent.[2]

Several forms of privatization were used (Kotrba and Svejnar, 1994): restitutions, small scale privatization, large scale privatization, direct transfers to municipalities and transformation of co-operative property. The relative weights of different forms are shown in Table 8.1.

The first step was a restitution programme: returning property to former owners (during 1990–92). It allowed the natural restitution of property that was expropriated after the Communist takeover of 1948. Since a major part of the Czech (and Czechoslovak) economy was nationalized before 1948, natural restitution accounts for a relatively small

Table 8.1   Summary of weights of different forms of privatization (in 1998)

	Accounting value in billions of CZK		share (%)	
1. restitutions	130		7.71	
2. transfer to municipalities	350		20.75	
3. small-scale privatization	23		1.36	
4. large-scale privatization	934		55.36	
including voucher privatization		333		19.74
other methods		391		23.18
state owned (not privatized yet)		210		12.45
5. transformation of cooperatives	250		14.82	
total	1687		100	

Source: Estimates of Ministry of Finance, National Property Fund, Czech Statistical Office
Hospodárské noviny, 5. 3. 1999

fraction of the total property (in accounting value about 130 billions of Czech crowns out of total about 1700 billions.).

The property transferred by the law directly (free of charge) from state to municipalities accounts for about 350 billions of crowns.

So called small-scale privatization was officially closed in December 1993. The law permitted the sale or leasing of real and movable property possessed by state owned enterprises and federal, republican and local governments. Property in accounting value about 23 billions of CZK was sold in auctions.[3]

The most important form, considering the importance and size of privatized property, was so called large-scale privatization. Large-scale privatization was carried out through the following basic methods:

- transformation of a state-owned enterprise into a joint stock company and a transfer of shares;[4]
- direct sale to a predetermined buyer;
- public auction or public tender.

The voucher privatization programme, which offered citizens chances to purchase shares in large companies for a small registration fee had met with popular enthusiasm (see Table 8.2). Within two years (1993–94) nearly every Czech was a shareholder; indeed, the Czechs were the largest per capita shareholders of any country, including the United States (Schwartz, 1997).

Table 8.2 Number of individual shareholders accounts (in millions)[5]

	September 1994	September 1995	December 1996	December 1997	January 1999
Total number of accounts	7.26	7.4	7.3	5.9	3.95
Empty accounts	0.95	2	2.5	1.8	1.03
Individual shareholders	6.31	5.4	4.8	4.1	2.92

Source: Středisko cenných papírú

Voucher privatization was a game (Kotrba, 1995).[6] For a registration fee of 1,000 CZK (about 35 US dollars at that time) every Czech citizen over the age of 18 residing permanently in the former Czechoslovakia obtained a voucher book formally worth 1,000 points. Individual investors could allocate the investment points of their voucher book to one or more of the companies listed on supply side. The bidding for shares was organized in several rounds. Before each round the authorities announced for each company its share price (in investment points), the number of available shares and the extent of excess demand registered in the previous round. In the first round the price was set identically for all companies and it was adjusted individually for each enterprise thereafter. At the end of each round, the Center for Voucher Privatization and Ministry of Finance processed the bids: If the demand for shares of a given company was equal or less than the supply of shares, all orders were met at the price set for this round. The authorities then reduced the share price for excess supply companies. If demand exceeded supply, the demand was satisfied only partly or no transaction took place; the investment points were returned to their owners, and the authorities raised the share price for the following round. The prices were set according to a complex algorithm that was never revealed.

Originally the privatization game was designed for individual investors as players. But lacking access to relevant information they were not prepared for the game. To assist individual investors' choice Investment Privatization Funds (IPFs) were created. They became the major players in the game and also the major winners (Bohatá, 1998). IPFs were supposed to act as collective investors to diversify their portfolios to minimize the risk. Before the bidding individual investors could allocate entirety or parts of their voucher books to one of several IPFs and then become their shareholders. Successful advertisement campaign of IPFs encouraged the majority of individual investors to commit their voucher points (or voucher books) to IPFs (72 per cent of investment points in the first wave and 63 per cent in the second wave). The voucher privatization became a game dominated by IPFs and the role of individuals in voucher privatization has been marginalized.

Czech banks (mostly controlled by the state) have played a crucial role within the process of voucher privatization. They established investment companies, those investment companies established dozens of IFPs and these funds became the major players in both waves of voucher privatization. The major Czech banks themselves were subjects of voucher privatization, but at the same time the Fund of National Property retained over 40 per cent of shares in major Czech banks.[7]

To classify large-scale privatization outcomes we can consider the following sectors: the state (public) sector (state controlled companies); companies privatized by voucher method, companies privatized by standard methods (public auctions, public tenders, direct sales) to Czech owners, companies privatized by standard methods to foreign owners. Table 8.1 provides data about the weights of different forms of large scale privatization (at the end of 1998): voucher method accounts for 19.74 per cent of national property, standard methods (both to Czech and foreign owners) for 23.18 per cent and weight of state for 12.45 per cent (based on accounting value).

After transformation decline in 1991 to 1993, deepened by external shocks of Comecon collapse and division of the country, GDP started to grow in 1994 (Table 8.3). Privatization seemed to be successful. In 1996 the Czech government publicly announced that transition was over and that the post-transitionary period was underway.

Illusions began to vanish in 1997. Then, the Czech public first learned that several managers of the investment funds designed to invest the public's vouchers were instead systematically stealing from their own investors. The Czech Ministry of Finance has enumerated 15 techniques for stealing.[8]

It appears that the voucher privatization and standard privatization into the 'Czech hands' (mostly in credit) did not lead to restructuring and improving the performance of privatized firms. The biggest improvements in performance may be observed in the foreign-controlled sector (Table 8.4). This sector, representing about 16 per cent of the total industrial sales, grew by more than 3 per cent in the first half of 1998 and led industrial growth. Foreign investors have been permanently enhancing productivity which is currently 41 per cent above the average level in the remaining sectors. The worst results are

Table 8.3 Czech Republic 1990–99, basic macroeconomic indicators

	Real growth rate of GDP	Rate of inflation (CPI)	Rate of unemployment	Balance of current account (in % of GDP)
1990	−1.2	9.7	1.0	−1.1
1991	−11.5	56.6	4.1	4.5
1992	−3.3	11.1	2.6	−1.0
1993	0.6	20.8	3.5	1.3
1994	3.2	10.0	3.2	−2.0
1995	6.4	9.1	2.9	−4.4
1996	3.9	8.8	3.5	−7.0
1997	1.0	8.5	5.2	−6.2
1998	−2.7	10.7	7.5	−1.9
1999[a]	−0.8	3.6	10.8	−2.7

[a] Estimate of Ministry of Finance, May 1999

Source: Zpráva vlády o stavu české společnosti (The Government Report), *Hospodárské noviny*, 5. 3. 1999, *Countries in Transition 1998, WIIW Handbook of Statistics*, Vienna 1998.

Table 8.4 Comparison of performance of sectors by method of privatization used in manufacturing industry (value added per one employee in thousands of CZK)

	1997	1998	% sales 98
Public/state sector[a]	360.9	465.6	16.5
Firms privatized by voucher method	277.2	321.5	23.4
Firms privatized by standard methods[b]	306.5	343.9	8.1
Sector under foreign control	680.3	743.2	16.3
other[c]	318.1	373.2	35.7
total over industry	326.4	389.2	100.0

[a] State enterprises, state controlled joint stock companies, municipal enterprises.
[b] Public auctions, public tenders, direct sales.
[c] Mixed or non-identifiable forms of privatization.

Source: Zpráva vlády o stavu české společnosti (The Government Report), *Hospodárské noviny*, 5. 3. 1999.

exhibited by firms privatized by the voucher method (they are behind the state sector firms).

The methods of privatization used generated a highly non-transparent ownership structure, led to 'fuzzy' design of corporate governance (Bohatá, 1998) and (in the absence of prudential regulation of capital markets and the banking sector) contributed to a slow-down of the economic performance of the Czech economy after 1996. It was not the only factor of post-privatization depression, but certainly the significant one.[9]

While expectations, raised by the blue-print of the privatization strategy, associated with the Civic Democratic Party of Václav Klaus, paved the way to an impressive victory for the right-centre coalition in the 1992 election (Turnovec, 1995), post-privatization depression went hand by hand with growing political instability.

Since 1992 the government coalition has consisted of three right-centrist parties: the Civic Democratic Party (ODS), the Christian-Democratic Union (KDU-CSL) and the Civic Democratic Alliance (ODA). After the 1996 parliamentary election these three parties formed a minority coalition government, controlling 99 of 200 seats in the Lower House and 53 of 81 seats in the Upper House. The minority coalition was tolerated by the social democrats, who abstained in the confidence vote. Out of 16 government offices, eight were held by the ODS, four by the KDU-CSL and four by the ODA.

Voters' preferences for political parties significantly changed during 1997. This was an expression of the growing criticism of the political and social development of the Czech Republic and of the economic problems that for a long time were neglected by the ruling coalition. Restrictive economic policies introduced in the spring of 1997 were accompanied only by cosmetic personnel changes in government. False expectations, raised by overly optimistic government propaganda, were dashed by economic recession, a decrease in real incomes, the exchange rate crisis, and the crisis in the banking sector.

In November 1997 the culmination of these problems led to the dissolution of the government coalition. During the Prime Minister's absence from the country, the two smaller parties, the ODA and KDU-CSL withdrew from the coalition and, after President Havel's intervention the government resigned on 30 November. While the immediate reason for the government crisis was related to the unclear financing of the Civic Democratic Party, indicating possible corruption during privatization, the November collapse of the government reflected the general instability of the Czech political environment. Feelings of dissatisfaction held by a substantial portion of the population regarding recent economic development, disapproval of the leading coalition party's political style, friction among coalition parties, and power struggles among different segments of the Czech political establishment contributed to the fall of the government.

Observing growing animosity among politicians and the inability of political parties to agree on the composition of a viable government,

President Havel appointed Mr Josef Tošovský, the generally respected Governor of the Czech National Bank with no party affiliation, as the new prime minister on 17 December 1997. The new government, not based on the parliamentary power of political parties, but supported by two small former coalition partners of the Civic Democratic Party (The Christian Democratic Union and Civic Democratic Alliance), was appointed by the President on 30 December 1997. After complicated negotiations and an explicit commitment by the government to hold new parliamentary elections in the spring of 1998, the government received the support of the Lower House of the Parliament on 28 January 1998, despite the opposition of the Civic Democratic Party, but with the unanimous approval of the Social Democrats.

In January 1998 the Civic Democratic Party split and the members who opposed Chairman Klaus's interpretation of the political crisis as a coup against the party and against him personally left the party and established a new party called the Union of Freedom.

Economic recession continued in 1998. With a limited mandate the 'provisional government' of Mr Tošovský, while praised by the public, did not have enough authority to initiate significant changes in economic policies. The June 1998 election of the Lower House failed to provide any clear answers.

While the Czech Social Democratic Party achieved historical success as the party with the strongest popular support (almost one-third of the voters cast their votes for the CSSD), the Civic Democratic Party demonstrated its skill in political tactics and ranked as the second strongest party, losing only 2 per cent of electoral support compared with the 1996 election. Shortly after the election President Havel authorized the chairman of the Social Democrats, Mr Zeman, to negotiate the composition of the new government. The Social Democrats failed to compose a left-centre majority coalition with the Christian and Democratic Union and the Union of Freedom. On the other hand, personal animosity among the leaders of the former coalition partners, the Civic Democratic Party, the Christian and Democratic Union and the Union of Freedom, prevented the establishment of a right centre majority coalition. A grand coalition of the CSSD and ODS was explicitly excluded by the electoral programmes of both parties. A resolution to the dead-lock was found in the so-called 'opposition treaty' between the CSSD and ODS. The ODS committed itself to tolerating a minority one party government of CSSD in exchange for a dominating role in the Lower and Upper Houses and participation in preliminary consultations on important issues between the CSSD and ODS. Having together a constitutional majority in the both houses of parliament, the CSSD and ODS declared their intention to work together to stabilize the Czech political environment. The abstention of the ODS in the confidence vote allowed the one party minority government of CSSD to receive the support of the Lower House in August 1998.

It is not the ambition of this paper to answer fully the question 'what had gone wrong'. It rather addresses the following problem: Considering non-transparency to be a market imperfection contributing to market failures, how we can measure 'transparency' or 'non-transparency' of an ownership structure, generated by method of privatization used?

2   Transparency of an ownership structure

Let us consider two types of economic agents: the primary owners, who can own, but cannot be owned (citizens, citizens' non-profit associations, state, municipalities etc.), and the secondary owners, who can be owned and at the same time can own (companies, corporations).

Let

m   be the number of primary owners, $i = 1, 2, \ldots, m$,
n   be the number of secondary owners (companies), $j = 1, 2, \ldots, n$,
s^0_{ji} be the direct share of primary owner i in secondary owner j (as a proportion of total number of shares),
t^0_{jk} be the direct share of the secondary owner (company) k in the secondary owner (company) j.

Then the $n \times m$ matrix

$$S_0 = (S^0_{ji})$$

where the row j expresses shares of the primary owners $i = 1, 2, \ldots, m$ in the secondary owner j, and the column i expresses the shares of the primary owner i in the secondary owners $j = 1, 2, \ldots, n$, will be called a matrix of primary property distribution, and the $n \times n$ matrix

$$T_0 = (T^0_{jk})$$

where the row j expresses shares of the secondary owners $k = 1, 2, \ldots, n$ in the secondary owner j, and the column j expresses shares of secondary owner k in the secondary owners $j = 1, 2, \ldots, n$, will be called a matrix of secondary property distribution. The couple

$$\{S_0, T_0\}$$

characterizes an initial property distribution in an economy. Clearly

$$\sum_{i=1}^{m} s_{ji}^0 + \sum_{k=1}^{n} t_{jk}^0 = 1$$

for any $j = 1, 2, \ldots, n$.

If $T_0 = 0_{nn}$, where 0_{nn} is the $n \times n$ zero matrix, we have a very simple and transparent structure, when only primary owners own companies and there exists no cross-ownership. However in real economies we need not have such transparent structures, and that can lead to situations when it is not so easy to see who owns what. If a primary owner A has a share in a secondary owner B, secondary owner B has a share in secondary owner C, and secondary owner C has a share in secondary owner D, then there exist direct ownership relations between A and B and B and C, and indirect ownership relations between A and C, A and D and B and D. If moreover D has a share in B, then the situation is completely unclear. The problem is how to evaluate direct and indirect property relations, and to identify the part of company C which is owned by primary owner A etc.

Assuming $T_0 \neq 0_{nn}$ let us consider a primary owner i. Clearly, his total share in the company (secondary owner) j is given not only by his direct share s_{ij}^0 in j, but also by the indirect share following from the shares of secondary owner j in the other companies. This can be expressed as

$$s_{ji}^1 = s_{ji}^0 + \sum_{k=1}^{n} t_{jk}^0 s_{ki}^0$$

Consider a secondary owner k. His effective share in the company j is given by appropriate fractions of the shares of the company j in other companies and by fractions of shares of other companies which he co-owns, in company j:

$$t_{jk}^1 = \sum_{r=1}^{n} t_{jr}^0 t_{rk}^0$$

In matrix form we have

$$S_1 = S_0 + T_0 S_0 \quad T_1 = T_0 T_0 = T_0^2$$

So, considering cross-ownership relations, we can obtain a decomposition of property on direct (following from registered shares of primary owners) component and indirect component (following from cross-ownership relations). We shall call distribution (S_0, T_0) a distribution of zero degree, and the distribution (S_1, T_1) a distribution of the first degree.

Now we have a new distribution $(\mathbf{S}_1, \mathbf{T}_1)$ taking into account indirect relations, and we can repeat all our procedures to produce a distribution of the second degree as

$$S_2 = S_1 + T_1 S_1 = (S_0 + T_0 S_0) + T_0^2(S_0 + T_0 S_0)$$

$$T_2 = T_1 T_1 = T_0^4$$

etc.. In the general case

$$S_r = S_{r-1} + T_{r-1} S_{r-1}$$

$$T_r = T_{r-1} T_{r-1}$$

$(r = 1, 2, \ldots k, \ldots)$.

Within the framework of this model the sequence of matrices $T_0, T_1, T_2, \ldots$ can be used for quantification of the concept of transparency of a property distribution (Turnovec, 1999).

If we accept as an axiom that finally any distribution of property is distribution among the primary owners only, then transparency of a particular distribution can be measured by the distance of primary distribution from the final distribution taking into account all degrees of indirect links.

Maximum transparency is achieved when $T_0 = 0_{nn}$. In this case primary distribution is transparent in the sense that any property is related to primary owners only and no indirect relations appear.

We shall say that a particular property structure (S_0, T_0) such that $T_0 \neq 0_{nn}$ is k-transparent, if in property distribution (S_k, T_k) of degree k it holds that $T_k = 0_{nn}$, while in property distribution of degree $k-1$ (S_{k-1}, T_{k-1}) it holds that $T_{k-1} \neq 0_{nn}$.

A property structure is non-transparent, if for any positive integer k it holds that $T_{k-1} \neq 0_{nn}$. Even in this case we can, however, identify an 'almost final' distribution of the property among the primary owners, but only in limit, because $T_0 < E$ where E is the matrix of 1s implies that

$$\lim_{k \to \infty} T_k = 0_{nn}$$

It can be proved that if T_0 is a square matrix of the order n such that the sequence of matrices T_0, $T_1 = T_0^2$, $T_2 = T_1^2 = T_0^4, \ldots$ converges to zero matrix, then either there exists k such that $2^k \leq n$ and $T_k = 0_{n \times n}$, or $T_r \neq 0_{nn}$ for any integer r.[10]

3 An application: How transparent is the Czech banking sector?

Tables 8.5, 8.6, 8.7, and 8.8 give an analysis of property structure of the core of the banking sector in the Czech Republic (end of 1997). There are five major banks, representing almost 90 per cent of the total assets of the Czech banking sector (Matoušek, 1998):

CS   Ceská sporitelna (Czech Saving Bank),
CP   Ceská pojišt'ovna (Czech Insurance),
KB   Komercní banka (Commercial Bank),
IPB   Investicní a poštovní banka (Investment and Post Bank),
CSOB   Ceskoslovenská obchodní banka (Czecho-Slovak Trade Bank).

As primary public owners we have:

FNM   Fond národního majetku (Fund of National Property), state agency,
CNB   Ceská národní banka Czech National Bank), central bank,
MF   Ministerstvo financí (Ministry of Finance), state agency,
Mun.   Sdruzení mest (Association of Municipalities),

Primary private owners are:

BH   Bank Holding, non-state,
JRING   J. Ring stock comp., non-state,
PPFI   First Privatization Holding, non-state,
BNY   The Bank of New York,
Nomura Nomura Group,
MB   The Midland Bank,
BTI   The Bankers Trust Investment,
SR   Slovak Republic,
others minority investors (mostly from voucher privatization).

The secondary owners are:

SPIF-C Sporitelní privatizacní investicní fond – Ceský (investment fund),

Table 8.5 Primary property distribution in the banking sector of the Czech Republic, end of 1997 (%)

	Primary owners (matrix S_0)													Secondary owners (matrix T_0)											
	FNM	CNB	MF	Mun.	BH	JRING	PPF1	BNY	No-mura	MB	BTI	SR	others	CS	CP	KB	IPB	CSOB	SPIF-C	SPIF-V	PPF	PIF	RIF	IPF-K	VS
CS	52.8				14.75								11.95		10.1	2.8			5.1	2.5					
CP	30.25												17.71	1.53			17.18	14			20.86				
KB	48.74							12.92					29.83									1.21	3.56	2.21	7.86
IPB	31.49				14.97				5.02				40.66												
CSOB	19.59	26.51	19.59									25.78	8.53												
SPIF-C										30			44.95	25.05											
SPIF-V										30	10		35.01	24.99											
PPF							100																		
PIF													86.2		13.8										
RIF	20.37												69.53		10.1										
IPF-KB													70.99			29.01									
VS				41.1	42.7								16.2												

Table 8.6 Property distribution of the first degree in the banking sector of the Czech Republic, end of 1997 (%)

	Primary owners (matrix S_1)														Secondary owners (matrix T_1)											
	FNM	CNB	MF	Mun.	BH	JRING	PPF	I	BNY	No-mura	MB	BTI	SR	others	CS	CP	KB	IPB	CSOB	SPIF-C	SPIF-V	PPF	PIF	RIF	IPE-K	VS
CS	57.22			14.75					0.36		2.28	0.25		17.7	1.95			1.74	1.41			2.1		0.1	0.6	1.35
CP	38.4	3.71	2.74	2.57			20.9			0.86			3.61	25.9		0.68	0.7									
KB	50.27			0.23					12.92					35.1						0.08	0.04					
IPB	31.49			18.2	3.36					5.02				41.9												
CSOB	19.59	26.51	19.59										25.78	8.53												
SPIF-C	13.23			3.69							30			47.9		2.53	0.7			1.28	0.63					
SPIF-V	13.19			3.69							30	10		38		2.52	0.7			1.27	0.62					
PPF								100																		
PIF	4.17													88.6				2.37	1.93			2.9				
RIF	23.43													71.3				1.74	1.41			2.1				
IPE-KB	14.14								3.75					79.6									0.4	1.03	0.64	
VS				41.1	42.7									16.2	0.44											

Table 8.7 Property distribution of the second degree in the banking sector of the Czech Republic, end of 1997 (%)

	Primary owners (matrix S₂)													Secondary owners (matrix T₂)											
	FNM	CNB	MF	Mun.	BH	JRING	PPF I	BNY	Nomura	MB	BTI	SR	others	CS	CP	KB	IPB	CSOB	SPIF-C	SPIF-V	PPF	PIF	RIF	IPF-K	VS
CS	59.19	0.37	0.28	15.04	0.32	0.06	2.1	0.37	0.09	2.32	0.25	0.36	19.1	0.04			0.04	0.03				0.000	0.000	0.026	0.0026
CP	38.4	3.71	2.74		3.13	0.58	20.9		0.86			3.61	26.1												
KB	50.89	0.03	0.02	0.23			0.1	13.01	0.0059	0.03	0.0038	0.02	35.6		0.076	0.005			0.002	0.000					0.009
IPB	31.49				18.2	3.36			5.02				41.9												
CSOB	19.59	26.51	19.59									25.78	8.53												
SPIF-C	14.8	0.09	0.07	3.77	0.07		0.5	0.09	0.02	30.57	0.06	0.09	49.7		0.05	0.000		0.002	0.002	0.01				0.03	0.03
SPIF-V	14.77	0.09	0.07	3.76	0.08		0.5	0.09	0.02	30.57	10.06	0.09	39.7		0.05	0.000		0.002	0.002	0.01				0.03	0.03
PPF							100																		
PIF	5.3	0.51	0.38		0.43	0.08	2.9		0.12			0.5	89.8												
RIF	24.25	0.37	0.28		0.32	0.06	2.1		0.09			0.36	72.2												
IPF-KB	14.74			0.07						0.01	0.0011		81.3	0.01			0.03	0.03				0.000	0.002	0.007	0.0044
VS					41.1	42.7	3.77			16.2															

Note: By 0.000 we indicate very small numbers close to zero.

Table 8.8 Property distribution of the third degree in the banking sector of the Czech Republic, end of 1997 (%)

	Primary owners (matrix S_3)													Secondary owners (matrix T_3)											
	FNM	CNB	MF	Mun.	BH	JRING	PPF1	BNY	No-mura	MB	BTI	SR	others	CS	CP	KB	IPB	CSOB	SPIF-C	SPIF-V	PPF	PIF	RIF	IPF-K	VS
CS	59.23	0.38	0.28	15.04	0.32	0.06	2.2	0.37	0.09	2.33	0.25	0.37	19.1	0.000				0.000	0.000			0.000	0.000	0.000	
CP	38.4	3.71	2.74		3.13	0.58	20.9	0.86				3.61	26.1			0.000	0.000			0.000					0.000
KB	50.9	0.03	0.02	0.23	0.02	0.004	0.1	13.01	0.0059	0.04	0.0039	0.02	35.8												
IPB	31.49			18.2	3.36				5.02				41.9												
CSOB	19.59	26.51	19.59									25.78	8.5		0.000	0.000			0.000	0.000		0.000	0.000	0.000	
SPIF-C	14.84	0.01	3.77		0.08	0.01	0.5	0.09	0.02	30.58	0.06	0.09	49.7		0.000	0.000			0.000	0.000				0.000	0.000
SPIF-V	14.8	0.01	3.76		0.08	0.01	0.5	0.09	0.02	30.58	10.06	0.09	39.8												
PPF							100																		
PIF	5.3	0.51	0.38	0.43	0.08		2.9		0.12			0.5	89.8												
RIF	24.25	0.37	0.28	0.32	0.06		2.1		0.09			0.36	72.2												
IPF-KB	14.77	0.0074	0.005		0.006	0.0000	0.000	3.77	0.0017	0.01	0.0011	0.0072	81.3												
VS				41.1	42.7								16.2	0.000				0.000	0.000			0.000	0.000	0.000	

Note: By 0.000 we indicate very small numbers close to zero.

SPIF-V   Sporitelní privatizacní investicní fond – výnosový (investment fund),
PPF   První privatizacní fond (investment fund),
PIF   První investicní fond (investment fund),
RIF   Restitucní investicní fond (investment fund),
IPF-K   Investicní privatizacní fond Komercní banky (investment fund),
VS   Vojenské stavby (stock company).

The structure is incomplete, because some of our primary owners are in fact secondary owners as well (owned mostly by foreign capital), but to have a closed system for illustrative purposes, we shall not go deeper.

Table 8.5 gives the primary distribution and then we present results of the three iterations considering different levels of indirect links (Table 8.6, property distribution of the first degree, Table 8.7 property distribution of the second degree, and Table 8.8 gives the property distribution of the third degree).

We can see that the state's shares were significantly higher taking into consideration indirect links than in the primary distribution, and that the system is non-transparent, because the powers of the matrix T_0 of primary distribution among secondary owners converge to zero matrix, but they will never be zero.

4   Concluding remarks

From the end of voucher privatization in 1994 until 1998, no significant progress was made in the transfer of state property into private hands. However, several interesting issues have arisen (Turnovec, 1998b).

So-called spontaneous privatization emerged during 1998. Financially strong groups have realized that after voucher privatization, state-owned companies exist with dispersed ownership in which the state's stake is below 50 per cent. These groups started massive yet silent buy-outs from investment funds and small private shareholders. As a result, they were able to collect a higher portion of stakes than was controlled by government agencies and therefore override the state's influence. Such takeovers were successful in the case of several firms operating in the coal mining industry, and there were attempts to take over other firms. A similar situation first occurred in 1997 when the 'Nomura Group' acquired a larger stake than the government in IPB. Nomura controlled more than 34 per cent and obtained veto power in the bank. Therefore, the government was left with Nomura as the only potential buyer.

Second, government officials took offensive action in response to the first few hostile takeovers. The National Property Fund has authorized co-operating brokerage houses to buy the shares of the remaining endangered companies, namely of utility distributors, to increase the state's stake to over 50 per cent in order to maintain control. This might be viewed as a step backward or as a corrective action to undo the wrongs of the previous privatization method.

As a reaction to the recession, the new Czech government of Social Democrats publicly announced its intention to 'revitalize' large industrial holding companies. The cabinet approved a final version of the industrial revitalization plan in April 1999. Fifteen to twenty collapsing firms of a national importance will probably be involved in the programme. It is estimated that about 200 million USD will be needed to help these companies survive. The restructuring will be controlled by the Revitalization Agency, which is staffed by deputies of the state-owned Consolidation Bank (Konsolidacní banka) and representatives from the financial sector. The Revitalization Agency will also find new strategic partners for selected companies or for their viable parts. The methods of the programme remain unclear; nevertheless, they would probably involve a combination of several instruments like debt for equity swaps (using non-performing loans), interest rate subsidies for selected firms, export guarantees, buyouts of certain debts and write-offs, and other standard and non-standard methods of industrial policy.

There has been a shift in the governmental privatization strategy towards favouring public tenders and direct sales to strategic investors, usually to strong multinational groups.

Finally, it was generally recognized, that the key issue is privatization of state-controlled banks. The first step was made in March 1998, when state share in IPB (Investment and Post Bank) was sold (for a nominal price) to Nomura Group. The second step followed in June 1999, when the most successful Czech Bank, CSOB (Czechoslovak Trade Bank), almost fully owned by state, was sold for one billion USD to Belgian KBC bank. Privatization of the state shares in the remaining two (most problematic) major Czech banks, CS (Czech Saving Bank) and KB (Commercial Bank) is expected in the year 2000.

The Czech experience shows that formally privatizing x per cent of former state property might still keep the state responsible for considerably more than $(100 - x)$ per cent. Resignation by the state from exercising property rights and the absence of a reasonable doctrine of temporary state capitalism contributed to the present problems of the Czech economy and Czech society (Schwartz, 1997).

Notes

1 This research was undertaken with support from the Grant Agency of the Academy of Sciences of the Czech Republic, project No. A8085901. The author is grateful to Marie Bohatá, Claudia Buch, Arye L. Hillman, and Bruno Schönfelder for valuable comments to earlier drafts of the paper.

2 Report of Ministry of Finance of the Czech Republic on the Law on Capital Market Regulation, 1997. For comparison: Hungary 25 per cent in 1990 and 75 per cent in 1996, Poland 31 per cent in 1990 and 78 per cent in 1996 (Turnovec, 1998a).

3 The revenues of the Fund of National Property (FNP) from auctions in small scale privatization exceeded 30 billion CZK, more than accounting value.

4 After the transformation of state-owned enterprises into joint-stock companies shares were distributed through a voucher privatization scheme to citizens, sold directly to a domestic of foreign owner, sold through an intermediary (stock exchange and other capital market instruments), sold to employees, issued to former owners as compensation, transferred free of charge to public institutions or municipal ownership. A significant part of the shares were transferred to the Fund of National Property representing state as an owner.

5 The shares are stored and updated electronically at individual investor's accounts in the Centre of Securities.

6 There were two waves of voucher privatization: the first wave in former Czechoslovakia (1991–92) and the second wave in the Czech Republic only (1993–94). Each wave was organized in several rounds.

7 A closed loop appeared: the state is controlling the bank; the bank owns the investment company; the investment company establishes several IPFs which control (on behalf of individual investors) hundreds of 'privatized' companies. The question arises: how much 'private' are formally privatized companies?

8 One of the common techniques: The investment fund managers sell company shares in the portfolio to dummy companies at absurdly cheap prices. The dummy companies sell the shares on the market. The dummy companies deposit the ensuing profits into overseas bank accounts. The fund investors are left with nothing.

9 Central bank (Czech National Bank, CNB) was heavily criticized for too restrictive monetary policies contributing to credit crunch (high interest rates, minimal reserve requirements) focused on exchange rate stability and inflation rate (Klaus, 1999), and for imperfections in regulation of the banking sector during the first years of transitions, and it cannot withdraw from its part of the responsibility for the recent problems in the country's economic development. But disputes about the responsibility of the CNB too frequently have strong political flavour and reflect a more general issue: how independent should the central bank be?

10 This statement follows from the theory of nilpotent matrices. A square $n \times n$ matrix A is called nilpotent to index k when $A_1^{k-1} 0_{nn}$ and $A^k = 0_{nn}$, k is a positive integer. It can be proved that if A is nilpotent to index k, then $k \leq n$ (Archibald, 1968).

References

Archibald, J. W. (1968) *Algebra*, London: Pitman Paperbacks.

Bohatá, M. (1998) Some Implications of Voucher Privatization for Corporate Governance, *Prague Economic Papers*, 7, 1, 44–58.

Klaus, V. (1999) *Zeme, kde se již dva roky nevládne*, Prague: CEP.

Kotrba, J. (1995) Privatization Process in the Czech Republic, in J. Svejnar (ed.), *The Czech Republic and Economic Transition in Eastern Europe*, San Diego: Academic Press, 59–98.

Kotrba J. and Svejnar, J. (1994) Rapid and Multifaced Privatization, Experience of the Czech and Slovak Republics, *MOST*, 4, 147–85.

Matoušek, R. (1998) Banking Regulation and Supervision: Lessons from the Czech Republic, *Prague Economic Papers*, 7, 1, 44–58.

Schwartz, A. (1997) Market Failure and Corruption in the Czech Republic, *Transition* (The World Bank), 8, 6, 4–5.

Turnovec, F. (1995) The Political System and Economic Transition, in J. Svejnar (ed.), *The Czech Republic and Economic Transition in Eastern Europe*, San Diego: Academic Press, 47–101.

Turnovec, F. (1998a) *Czech Republic 1997, The Year of Crises*, Prague: CERGE of Charles University and EI of Academy of Sciences of the Czech Republic.

Turnovec, F. (1998b) *Czech Republic 1998, Facing Reality*, Prague: CERGE of Charles University and EI of Academy of Sciences of the Czech Republic.

Turnovec, F. (1999) *Privatization, Ownership Structure, and Transparency: How to Measure the True Involvement of the State, European Journal of Political Economy*, 15, 605–618.

Countries in Transition 1998 (1998) WIIW Handbook of Statistics. The Vienna Institute for International Economic Studies, Vienna.

Zpráva vlády o stavu české společnosti, *Hospodárské noviny*, 5. 3. 1999.

9
Privatization, Ownership Structure and Transparency: Comment on František Turnovec

Claudia M. Buch

1   What is special about the Czech Republic?

When talking about the experience of the Czech Republic in the context of a conference on financial turbulences and financial markets in transition economies, one needs to ask if there are specific features of the Czech experience which make studying the case worthwhile. Although Mr Turnovec does not make this link explicit, he points implicitly at a key characteristic of the Czech 'system' which sets it apart from other countries. It is the failure to decisively reform institutions and corporate governance systems which has for all too long been hidden behind a curtain of macroeconomic success, but which now makes a recovery from a (comparatively) limited crisis in 1997 painful. In particular, Turnovec provides a very detailed account of the ownership structure in the Czech banking industry. Understanding the characteristics of this system of cross-ownership is crucial for understanding the system of corporate governance in the Czech Republic, the importance of which has often been overlooked prior to the 1997 crisis.

In these comments, rather than discussing the details of Turnovec's empirical approach, I am going to argue that the ownership pattern in the Czech financial system is a key factor behind financial market developments. Yet, macroeconomic developments need to be taken into account as well in order to distill the lessons from the Czech experience. In fact, the key note is the crucial role of the banking sector in providing sound domestic governance structures and in enhancing financial stability.[1]

In addition, the Czech Republic has been one the first countries in the region to suffer from a currency crisis in the aftermath of the Asian financial crises. For a long time, the Czech Republic's achievements were impressive. Unemployment rates remained by far the lowest in the region. Inflation has not exceeded single digits since 1994. The economy grew at 5 per cent in both 1995 and 1996 on the basis of comparatively high investment rates. These achievements appeared to be soundly based on a macroeconomic policy package involving balanced budgets, a tight monetary policy, and a nominal exchange rate fixed relative to a currency basket since 1991.

However, the current account deficit had been widening since 1994. Net capital in-flows, which had soared in 1994 and 1995, started to dwindle in 1996. Several policy measures designed to reduce the current account imbalance, such as the announcement of reduced government spending, remained ineffective. International investors attacked the fixed exchange rate. Within only a few days, the Central Bank suffered a massive loss of foreign currency reserves. On 27 May 1997, the Bank was forced to abolish the exchange rate target and to let the exchange rate float. The government subsequently plunged into disarray over austerity measures needed to correct both the external imbalance and domestic structural deficiencies. As a result, growth has slowed down considerably while inflationary pressure and unemployment have risen.

2   Why microeconomic factors matter

A crucial underlying reason for the runaway current account deficit was that productivity growth was generally weak, whereas wages have been allowed to grow rapidly both in real domestic and in dollar terms.[2] This points to problems with the governance of enterprises. Weak financial market regulation has reduced the transparency of ownership relations and has prevented the emergence of corporate governance structures conducive to the restructuring of firms. The role of banks is particularly important. On the one hand, banks have been assigned an influential role in the governance of firms via their fund management arms. On the other hand, (partial) state-ownership of the banks, a relatively high share of non-performing loans on their balance sheets, and weak regulations have reduced banks' incentives to efficiently monitor enterprises. Despite successive rounds of bank recapitalization, which aimed at reducing the burden of inherited bad assets, non-performing loans still stood at about 30 per cent of total loans in 1997 as compared to values at or even below 10 per cent in Poland or Hungary (EBRD, 1998, p. 133).

Turnovec's chapter provides an interesting account of the cross-ownership in the Czech banking sector and the problems that arise when trying to capture the true involvement of the state. Yet, in order to obtain a full picture of the implied incentive and governance structures, his analysis would have to be enriched by more evidence about the institutional background of the Czech governance system. Phrased differently, just as direct ownership links provide little evidence concerning the actual allocation of power, having information about indirect links is only a first step towards understanding the governance system as a whole. This, however, is crucial before deriving policy implications. Ultimately, governance structures must be thought of as systems of complementary and substitutional elements in which changing one element alone may not necessarily help to improve performance (Heinrich, 1999). Hence, the chapter could be clearer and go beyond the evidence on actual ownership structures and elude to the linkages between ownership structure and corporate governance. On a more practical level, one of the problems in the Czech Republic seems to be that not even information about the actual first order ownership distribution (both primary and secondary) may be available due to a significant amount of under-the-counter trade.

3   Why external liberalization matters

Microeconomic reforms, however important they may be, cannot substitute for sound macroeconomic policies. Hence, in order to understand the causes and consequences of the Czech financial crises of 1997, one also needs to take account of external financial liberalization and the role played by commercial banks in intermediating foreign capital.

Arguably, the Czech Republic has pursued one of the most liberal strategies of capital account liberalization of all transition economies, being outperformed only by, for instance, Estonia. With regard to capital inflows, foreign direct investment, except in specified sectors such as banking, was liberalized early on. Inward portfolio investment in bonds and equity is generally permitted but the placement of domestic securities abroad usually requires permission. Most importantly, however, the Czech Republic has shown a more liberal attitude with respect to short-term capital flows than countries like Hungary or Poland (Backé, 1996).

At the same time, the foreign exchange law allows the Central Bank to impose deposit requirements on inward capital flows for three months in times of severe balance of payments problems or to stop certain transactions entirely (CNB, 1995). While this safeguard clause was not used during the May 1997 crisis, the Central Bank did instruct commercial banks not to lend in koruna to nonresidents. Apparently, however, this instruction was not enforced strictly.[3] Somewhat contrary to the liberal regime with regard to capital flows, the Czech Republic followed a fairly restrictive policy with regard to the market entry of foreign banks during much of the transition period (Buch, 1997). As a result, market shares of foreign banks in the Czech Republic are below those of Hungary but above those observed in Poland. At the same time, Czech commercial banks have been important intermediaries and recipients of foreign capital. Net foreign assets of Czech banks had declined continuously in the years prior to the currency crises of 1997 but rebounded at the end of 1997, being driven mainly by an increase in gross foreign assets.

The comparatively liberal regime with regard to capital flows has been combined with an exchange rate regime less flexible than that of Hungary or Poland. After devaluing the koruna by a total of 70 per cent in 1990, a central parity to a basket of US-dollar and D-mark was maintained through spring 1997. The band within which the exchange rate was allowed to fluctuate was widened from 0.5 to 7.5 per cent on either side in February 1996 in response to large capital inflows which were swelling domestic money supply and creating inflationary pressures. Despite the ensuing nominal appreciation, expansionary wage policies and insufficiently tight fiscal policies caused a further widening of the already large current account deficit to unsustainable levels. Eventually, the currency crisis of 1997 forced the Central Bank to give up its exchange rate target, and a policy of a managed float combined with an inflation target has been followed recently.

Being comparatively open for foreign capital has potentially exposed the Czech Republic to negative effects of external financial crises. Ultimately, the question which capital flows are the most volatile remains an empirical one. As Table 9.1 shows, between 1993 and 1998 (net) short-term capital flows have been the most volatile item on the Czech balance of payments, measured by their coefficient of variation. Moreover, capital outflows (that is capital exports of residents) have been at least as volatile as capital imports. Yet, when distinguishing the level of capital flows before and after the crisis of 1997, it becomes evident that the greatest swing has occurred for long-term capital flows. Long-term inflows were substantial before the crisis but almost came to a halt after the crisis. Perhaps contrary to the conventional wisdom, portfolio investments have not necessarily been more volatile than 'other investments' (primarily loans and deposits). Overall, there is thus no consistent pattern of volatility of capital inflows

Table 9.1 Magnitude and volatility of capital flows 1993–98

	Average quarterly inflows (mil. US$)			Coefficient of variation		
	1993–98	1993–96	1997–98	1993–98	1993–96	1997–98
Current account	−424	−376	−533	−1.16	−1.40	−0.70
Financial account	935	1186	361	0.85	0.64	1.44
FDI (net)	335	328	350	0.93	1.10	0.41
Portfolio investment (net)	251	284	175	1.34	0.89	2.68
Other investment (net)	348	574	−165	1.87	0.85	−4.21
Short-term (net)	−19	49	−171	−30.10	8.82	−4.20
Inflow	662	717	535	0.85	0.67	1.30
Outflow	−680	−668	−707	−1.16	−0.64	−1.81
Long-term (net)	367	525	6	1.20	0.71	63.32
Inflow	364	492	73	0.68	0.43	1.40
Outflow	3	33	−67	40.71	3.08	−1.30

Source: Homepage of the Czech National Bank, own calculations.

– while FDI has been relatively stable, portfolio capital and other capital flows cannot unequivocally be ranked by volatility.

4   What are the lessons?

There are a number of lessons that other transition economies or other emerging markets can take from the Czech experience. In order to enjoy the beneficial effects of increased capital inflows while avoiding excessive real exchange rate appreciation and unsustainable current account deficits, appropriate policy responses must be taken. On the macroeconomic front, tightening monetary policy will do little by itself to cool off an economy and to reduce the current account imbalance. Raising short-term domestic interest rates, will further encourage short-term capital inflows and, with a fixed exchange rate, will swell money supply. Therefore, fiscal policy has a crucial role to play. As the Czech experience shows, governments may even have to go beyond limiting the size of budget deficits and may have to achieve a surplus instead. Moreover, rigid exchange rate targets can be invaluable in weaning an economy away from highly inflationary habits. But once significant headway has been made towards stabilization, and once foreign capital starts pouring in, monetary policy requires some added manoeuvring space, and a measure of flexibility should be added to the exchange rate target.

However, one of the most important lessons from the Czech experience is that macroeconomic factors alone are an imprecise and perhaps misleading indicator of the underlying strength of an economy. Rather, institutional and microeconomic conditions must be taken into account as well. Aside from the macroeconomic austerity measures introduced in the aftermath of the crisis, improving corporate governance is therefore particularly urgent. For this purpose, additional reforms in the banking sector are still necessary. Enhancing competitive pressure and efficiency by decisively opening up for foreign banks must be a key ingredient of a reform programme. In fact, the partial decoupling of capital account liberalization and of the abolishing of entry barriers for foreign commercial banks has not been conducive to ensuring an efficient allocation of financial funds and to enhancing information for foreign investors about the Czech market.

Because banks' weak incentives have eventually contributed to the poor performance of the Czech economy, the problems in the banking sector and the recent balance of payment crisis are merely two sides of the same coin. Few transition economies can claim to have truly sound banking sectors, and many are facing serious corporate governance problems of one sort or another. The larger point emanating from the Czech experience thus is that microeconomic weaknesses can derail even otherwise sound macroeconomic policies, and that addressing these weaknesses is crucial not only to prepare the ground for lasting economic growth, but also to preserve domestic and external balance in the short term.

Notes

1 These comments are based mainly on Buch and Heinrich (1997) as well as Buch, Heinrich and Pierdzioch (1999) which give accounts of the experiences of the Czech Republic and of other transition economies with external financial liberalization and which also review the literature on the issue.
2 See also OECD (1998). Smidkova (1998) finds evidence for a real exchange rate misalignment of the Czech crown in 1996.
3 Also, a special limit on the short-term open foreign exchange position of commercial banks *vis-à-vis* nonresidents was in place between August 1995 and October 1997 (IMF, 1998a).

References

Backé, P. (1996) Progress Towards Convertibility in Central and Eastern Europe. Österreichische Nationalbank, *Focus on Transition*, 1, 39–67.

Buch, C. M. (1997) Opening up for Foreign Banks – Why Central and Eastern Europe Can Benefit, *Economics of Transition*, 5, 2, 339–66.

Buch, C. M. and Heinrich, R. (1997) The End of the Czech Miracle? – Currency Crisis Reveals Need for Institutional Reforms, *Discussion Paper 301*, Kiel: Kiel Institute of World Economics.

Buch, C. M., Heinrich, R. and Pierdzioch, C. (1999) *Foreign Capital and Economic Transformation – Risks and Benefits of Free Capital Flows*, Kiel Study 295, Tübingen: Mohr.

Czech National Bank (CNB) (1995) *Devisengesetz*, 219/1995 der Gesetzessammlung vom 26 September 1995, Prague.

European Bank for Reconstruction and Development (EBRD) (1998) *Transition Report 1998 – Financial Sector in Transition*, London.

Heinrich, R. (2000) Corporate Governance – A Systemic Approach with an Application to Eastern Europe, in Wagener, H.-J. (ed.), *Privatization, Corporate Governance and the Emergence of Markets in Central-Eastern Europe*, Macmillan (forthcoming).

International Monetary Fund (IMF) (1998a) Czech Republic – Selected Issues. *IMF Staff Country Report 98/36*, Washington, DC: IMF.

International Monetary Fund (IMF) (1998b) *International Financial Statistics* (IFS) on CD-ROM, Washington, DC: IMF.

Organisation for Economic Co-operation and Development (OECD) (1998) *OECD Economic Surveys 1997–1998 (Czech Republic)*, Paris: OECD.

Smidkova, K. (1998) Estimating the FEER for the Czech Republic, *Czech National Bank Working Paper 87*, Prague.

10
Comment on František Turnovec

Bruno Schönfelder

This discussion consists of three parts. The first comments on the formal analysis presented by Dr Turnovec. The second deals with the broader issues raised in the introduction and the concluding remarks of his paper. The third shortly discusses the remarks of Dr Buch. These remarks contain some critical views on Czech reforms which are currently rather popular but in my view fallacious.

1 Remarks on the formal model

František Turnovec has provided us with an elegant and lucid analysis. Transparency of ownership structures is a frequent request which is brought up by many including for example the German monopoly commission who only recently complained about the intransparent ownership structures of numerous German companies.[1] Typically, the terms transparency and intransparency are used in a vague sense. Turnovec has made an effort to spell out what seems to be meant by complainants. This is valuable because it might incite them to reconsider their preconceptions. However, as is frequently the case with formal analysis, one of its merits is that it instils doubts about what has been shown.

Dr Turnovec's numerical examples suggest that his measure of intransparency displays the somewhat awkward property that k-transparency with k less than infinity is likely to be a rare case. A trifle of interlocking ownership apparently suffices to drive the measure up to infinity. His calculations for Czech banks provide an illustration of this problem. The second degree property distribution which he calculates tells us nearly everything. Further iterations result only in negligible changes. Nevertheless the measure k of transparency is infinity, indicating total intransparency. Presumably this problem can be fixed by refining the measure somewhat. Maybe one should specify that the distribution is k-transparent if after the k-th iteration all of the elements of the matrix T are in some sense 'close enough' to zero.

However, I am not sure that even such a refined measure of transparency would measure something which is of real economic significance. Transparency of ownership structures as defined by this measure and social welfare presumably are unrelated. It has been shown that at least in some cases intransparent ownership structures like cross ownership might be welfare-enhancing and superior to more transparent ownership structures. In the literature, we can find formal models which demonstrate this. Four cases are of particular relevance. First, 'intransparent' varieties of ownership provide a vehicle for diversifying risks. This is a productive activity provided that diversification does not dilute incentives 'excessively'. Second, cross-ownership affords protection against unfriendly take-overs. Sometimes such protection is welfare-enhancing.[2] I believe that this is a particularly relevant argument for economies in transition.[3] Third, cross-ownership can support long-term relations and enable the involved parties to invest in relation-specific assets without running the risk of a hold-up. This may be welfare-enhancing in particular if other means of protecting such assets like vertical integration or detailed contracts are difficult to establish.[4] Fourth, complicated ownership structures may enhance managerial independence which may be particularly desirable if the ultimate owner happens to be the government. To illustrate, Turnovec shows that until the full privatization of IPB (Investiční a poštovni banka) in spring 1998, FNM (Fond narodniho majetku) ultimately owned nearly 40 per cent of ČP (Česká pojišťovna), but only 30 per cent directly – the rest was owned indirectly via IPB. In IPB itself governement had only a minority position. As far as politicians' ability to influence ČP's management is concerned, indirect ownership obviously is not the same as direct ownership, in particular since government could not fully control IPB. Thus, in some respect intransparency contributes towards a depolitization of management, which in my view is desirable. Summarizing, we might conclude that equating transparency and good governance is overly simplistic.

2   The broader issues

Next, I will turn to some issues mentioned (in passing) in the conclusion and the introduction to Dr Turnovec's paper. In his introduction, he appears to endorse views that 'voucher privatization did not contribute to restructuring and improving the performance of privatized firms'. Currently, voucher privatization is being criticized by many observers, and some, like the Czech vice premier Mertlik, even claim that it was the main mistake committed in the course of Czech economic reforms. At the very best, such claims are overstated. The Coase theorem suggests that the way in which privatization proceeds is of rather limited importance for efficiency, what matters most is whether resources do actually become private property. In this view, the debate as to which privatization technique contributes most to enhancing efficiency, is largely a waste of time.[5] It follows that the choice between privatization techniques should first be based upon political considerations, particularly upon what is likely to be acceptable to the public and strengthen public support for the institution of private ownership. On this score, Czech privatization does not fare so badly. Maybe the most convincing evidence for this hypothesis is the observation, that as of now all democratic parties in the Czech republic including the social democrats agree that the privatization of all major banks should be completed as soon as possible. Such a consensus constitutes remarkable progress and could by no means be taken for granted considering that major parts of the social democrats until recently expressed sympathy for ideas like workers' self-management and third ways and wanted to keep most banks in state hands for a long time, if not forever.[6]

Evidence such as that presented in Table 8.2 of the Turnovec chapter should be interpreted with great caution. A high value added per employee in the state sector is not so surprising if one considers that the most significant state-owned companies are the electricity and the telephone company (and the railway system), companies which should have a high value-added per employee. Moreover, foreign investors have been interested only in the best companies and were able to provide substantial know-how and investment. As a result, their high value added is hardly surprising. The difference between voucher privatized firms and those privatized by standard methods is not so significant and might also be explainable by initial selection bias. Indeed, this hunch is supported by a more extensive version of this table which includes 1996.[7] Table 8.2 certainly does not prove the claim that voucher privatization was a failure. Indeed, if one focuses on growth rates and considers the more extensive version, one might just as well 'conclude' that voucher privatization has resulted in an above-average improvement. Irrespective of what one thinks about this table, it is undisputable that most voucher privatized companies have increased their productivity and have engaged in some restructuring.

In his concluding remarks Turnovec suggests that Czech privatization in some sense transformed a transparent variety of public property into an intransparent variety. Moreover, he seems to endorse criticisms that blame the Klaus government for rarely exercising state property rights. Managers of companies partly owned by the state rarely received orders from the government, neither were they monitored closely.

A comparative note might be useful at this point. Extensive interlocking shareholderships involving among others partly or fully state-owned companies have been a wide-spread phenomenon in countries such as France, Italy, Germany, Sweden, Austria and others for decades. Large companies such as Hochtief, TUI, Preussag and many others are indirectly co-owned by German government. I very much doubt, that Germany would be better off if these indirect and intransparent state holdings would be transformed into a more transparent form of public property for example by organizing a state holding company and if the German government would start to make an active use of its ownership rights.

Let us take another example. I believe that we can see parallels between the way the Czech government and the French government have treated CEOs of state-owned firms. In either case, government has rarely interfered with management decisions, by and large management has enjoyed a very considerable degree of autonomy.[8] The French record does not suggest that this is the worst way to deal with state-owned companies. Dr Turnovec endorses a criticism voiced against the Klaus government that it did not have a reasonable doctrine of temporary state capitalism. It seems to me that there was some sort of a doctrine and its major message was not to interfere with management decisions except if problems became very serious. I tend to believe that this is not so unreasonable.

Klaus' statement that the Czech republic has completed transformation has frequently been quoted and criticized, but for the sake of fairness one might want to add that it was made during a campaign and that he qualified it later, after the campaign was over.[9] According to his qualification, he did not mean to claim that the Czech economy has already turned into a fully fledged and smoothly functioning free enterprise economy. He rather wanted to say that the period of rapid change was over, any further progress towards the goal of a fully fledged free enterprise economy unavoidably would be slow-paced. So, he identified transformation with rapid change.

Turnovec claims that asset stripping (tunelovani) by mutual fund managers was 'formally legal'. This touches upon a difficult issue which presumably deserves to be worked out in much more detail. The Czech investment company act was reformed numerous times. In my reading, the very first version enacted in May 1992, contains some notion of fiduciary duty and calls on regulatory authorities to penalize managers who cheat investors. At the very least, it is less than obvious that tunelovani is legal under this act. A legislator unavoidably has the problem that at the time of writing a law he simply cannot know how courts and regulatory authorities will use and interpret it. Meanwhile, the legislator has reacted to ensuing problems by regulating in ever-growing detail what constitutes a breach of fiduciary duties. However, it does not follow that he should have tried to do this from the very beginning, considering the unavoidably limited knowledge and competence of both the ministries in charge and the legislating authority, the parliament. If it were true, that cheating became the norm and honest behaviour a rare exception among mutual fund managers, one might argue with some justification that the legislator should have proceeded more cautiously. Unfortunately, we have very little quantitative information about the amount of tunelovani. Casual empiricism suggests that cheating did not become the norm, even though it was not a rare event either.

3   Critical comments on the discussion by Claudia Buch

In my view, some of the critical remarks which Dr Buch voices against Czech economic policies are misguided. Due to limits of space I have to confine myself to a few notes.

Institution building takes time; the fact that the institutions of capitalism do not yet function smoothly in the Czech republic does not prove that nothing has been achieved. Accusing the Czech government of a 'failure to decisively reform institutions' is unfair to the heroic efforts which have been undertaken. Adherents to such critical views frequently pinpoint alleged failures of corporate government and the banking system. In my view, they stress the wrong issues. To be more specific, consider the three large industrial companies which are in severe trouble now, Chemapol, Škoda Plzen and ČKD. The crisis of these three large systems overshadows the much better performance of a myriad of small and medium-sized enterprises. These three companies have many problems, but it is less than clear that they are of the nature of corporate governance problems. All of them have an ownership structure which provides managers with high-powered incentives. For example, Lubomír Soudek, the CEO of Škoda is a 20 per cent block-holder. Thus, there is no

separation of ownership and control, which could give rise to governance problems, rather ownership is highly concentrated and a lot is at
risk for the owner Soudek. Similarly, the managements of Chemapol and
ČKD own substantial blocks of the shares of the respective companies.[10]
The fact that performance is unconvincing in spite of tough incentive
structures, reminds us that incentives (governance) are not the only
factor that counts. These managers did undertake considerable efforts
towards restructuring their companies, which, however, were less successful than had been hoped.

The aforementioned three companies have also been considered as
examples for lax lending policies of banks. Again, it is not so clear that
this indictment is fully justified. ČKD and Chemapol have frequently
complained about banks' reluctance to grant them credit. According to
the CEO of ČKD, banks provide credit only 'by drops'.[11] Different from
ČKD, which has been regarded as an ailing[12] company for many years,
the CEOs both of Škoda and Chemapol were widely regarded as among
the most competent Czech managers. Thus, it is not so incomprehens-
ible why in the end banks lent them substantial amounts.

In retrospect, one may easily conclude that banks engaged in very
risky business, which a conservative Western European banker might
have shied away from. However, contrary to Buch I do not believe that
this kind of behaviour is indicative of 'weak incentives' or misinterme-
diation. Banking in transition differs substantially from 'normal' banking, it somewhat resembles running a venture-fund. In particular, during
the first years of transition, standard techniques for evaluating risks as
used by banks elsewhere are nearly inapplicable. Under such circumstances, normal 'conservative' banking would result in a credit crunch,
banks would finance only a very limited number of projects, they would
prefer to buy public bonds, offer some consumptions loans and invest
most of their remaining funds abroad. Such banks would fail to fulfil
their major task which is intermediating funds. The observation that
Czech banks hold a significant stock of nonperforming assets which is
larger than in Poland or Hungary does not establish proof that the Czech
banking system had a more severe corporate governance problem. A
major difference between the Czech financial system and the other
aforementioned countries is that the share both of deposits and credits
in the Czech GDP is much larger than in Poland or Hungary. Moreover,
as a result of relatively small fiscal deficits Czech banks had less opportunity to invest in public bonds. Thus, the supply of safe investment
opportunities for Czech bankers was quite limited. Thus, it is easy to
understand that they could hardly avoid engaging in rather risky

business. There is evidence, that they nevertheless tried to be cautious. Such evidence is provided, for example, by the observation that during phases of vigorous base money expansion (1994–95) the money multiplier was small and unstable. Expansion of credit and sight deposits lagged notably behind the expansion of base money.[13]

The parallel between banking in transition and the operation of a venture fund also invalidates Buch's proposition that foreign banks should have been allowed to enter the Czech market earlier and on a larger scale. If one expects that banks finance very risky investment one must also enable them to earn rents on those investments which turn out as successful.[14] This is not possible if competition for good clients becomes too tough because foreign banks have entered the market on a large scale. In my view, in the first years of transition it is quite advisable to limit competition between banks. Otherwise competition for good clients may become excessive. Such excessive competition would not result in an improvement of banks' performance but in a large bill for the tax payer who would have to bail out domestic banks in the end.

I also disagree with Buch's evaluation of macromanagement. She proposes that in 1995–96 the Czech government should have prevented overheating by implementing more restrictive fiscal policies. She endorses the opinion that Czech fiscal policies were lax because the (consolidated) budget was not really balanced. In my view, Czech fiscal policies have been fairly restrictive ever since 1990. Standard macroeconomics suggests that fiscal impact should be evaluated not only on the basis of the fiscal deficit, a similarly significant variable is the overall size of public revenue and public expenditure. It is noteworthy that the share of (consolidated) public expenditure in the Czech GDP declined from 46.2 per cent in 1993 to 42.1 per cent in 1996 and less than 40 per cent in 1998. Considering that the (consolidated) fiscal deficit did not exceed 3 per cent until 1997, these figures suggest a rather restrictive fiscal stance.[15] Suggesting that fiscal policy should have been even more restrictive does not make much sense, since there are obvious political limits to how restrictive fiscal policies can be. This is not to dispute that more should have been done to prevent overheating. In the aftermath of overheating and the subsequent financial crisis the Czech National Bank implemented very restrictive policies which later turned out as overly restrictive and have meanwhile caused a recession. Thus, in retrospect we recognize that Czech macromanagement has fallen into a stop-and-go pattern. Since in 1994–96 the task of preventing overheating could not be handled by fiscal policy alone, fiscal policy was overcharged, we should look for alternative policy instruments. At least one candidate is available. After all overheating was largely due to excessive capital inflows. In my view, the Czech government liberalized capital flows too early. Moreover, it might have been wise to go off the fixed exchange rate earlier – in 1995 rather than in 1997.

Notes

1 Ordnungspolitische Leitlinien für ein funktionsfähiges Finanzsystem. Sonder-gutachten 26. Baden-Baden: Nomos, 1998, p. 79.
2 See Sten Nyberg (1995) Reciprocal Shareholding and Takeover Deterrence, *International Journal of Industrial Organization*, 13, pp. 335–72 and Mike Burkart, Denis Grob and Fausto Panunzi (1997) Large Shareholders, Monitoring and the Value of the Firm, *The Quarterly Journal of Economics*, 112, pp. 693–727.
3 A more extensive discussion of this issue is to be found in my Auf dem Weg zum besten Wirt ? Anmerkungen zur Entwicklung der Eigentumsverhältnisse in der tschechischen Industrie, *Osteuropa-Wirtschaft*, 1, 1999 (in print). The reader who is interested in a more detailed treatment of some other issues touched upon in this discussion might want to consult this paper.
4 This issue has been discussed extensively in the large literature on Japanese companies.
5 A more extensive exposition of this view is beyond the scope of this discus-sion. In most if not all transition countries we observe that in the post-privatization stage ownership structures tend to change rather quickly and substantially. This seems to occur irrespective of the method of privatization. Fears that some privatization methods might result in a freeze of ownership structures have proved wrong even in Russia where ownership transfers are far more difficult to effect than in the Czech Republic. Such observations suggest that 'transaction costs' are not so high and that the Coase theorem, resultantly, holds. For relevant evidence on Russia see S. Aukucionek, V. Žukov and V. Kapeljušnikov (1998) Dominirujušcie kategorii sobstvennikov i ich vlijanie na chozjajstvennoe povedenie predprijatij, *Voprosy ekonomiki*, 12, pp. 108–28.
6 Moreover, one might note that German, Austrian or Italian politicians, unfor-tunately, are far from being able to reach a similar consensus on privatizing banks. In this regard, the Czech Republic is considerably ahead of us.
7 A more extensive version of this table can be found in *Ekonom*, 4, 1999, p. 29. The reader might notice that the table suffers from a number of defects. First, to what it precisely refers is not clear. Second, the method of grouping is also unclear, since a rather typical pattern of Czech privatization which applied to many companies was that one part of the stock of the company was privatized by means of voucher privatization, another by means of 'standard methods' and another part remained in state hands. So, how do you group such a 'mixed' company?
8 A useful narrative on France can be found in Jonathan Charkham (1994) *Keeping Good Company*, Oxford: Oxford University Press.
9 See Vaclav Klaus (1997) Reflexe nedávného ekonomického vývoje, *Ekonom*, 48, pp. 22–3.

10 The management of Chemapol holds a 9 per cent block, most of the rest used to be owned by the banks. At the time of writing, one individual, the entrepreneur Radim Masný, owns 44 per cent of the Chemapol-holding. Thus, ownership of Chemapol is even more concentrated than that of Škoda Plzen. This is remarkable, considering the fact that Chemapol is among the largest companies of the Czech republic. Forty-one per cent of ČKD are owned by Inpro, a firm owned by the management of ČKD.

11 See Restrukturalizace bude bolet, *Ekonom*, 30, 1997, p. 15 and Interview with Václav Junek in *Ekonom*, 2, 1998.

12 Ailing but not hopeless as is indicated by the fact that most of the remaining stock has been owned by institutional investors from abroad

13 See Tomáš Holub (1997), Peněžní multiplikátor a menový vývoj v ČR, *Finance a úver*, 47, 3, pp. 129–42. Otherwise the Czech Central Bank would have experienced even more difficulty dealing with strong capital inflows in those years.

14 This intuition was formalized, for example, by Jean-Paul Pollin and Anne-Gaël Vaubourg (1998) L'architecture optimale des systèmes financiers dans les pays émergents, *Revue économique*, 49, 1, pp. 223–38.

15 These data are taken from Jan Kubín (1997) Analýza vývoje verejných rozpočtu ČR v letech 1993–1996, *Finance a úver*, 47, 47, p. 478. There is considerable controversy about the appropriate measures of public revenue, public expenditure and the fiscal deficit in the Czech Republic. However, the basic trends of a declining share of both public revenue and public expenditure are pronounced enough to remain intact throughout the controversy. It is worth noting that before 1993 and in particular before 1990 the share of public expenditure was much higher than now.

11

The Assessment of the Costs and Benefits of the Small and Medium Commercial Banks within the Czech Banking Sector[1] – Supplementary Chapter to František Turnovec

Roman Matoušek and Anita Taci

1 Introduction

Taking the transition countries as a whole, there have been several distinct stages leading to gradual improvement of internal efficiency and optimal resource allocation within the banking sectors, or in other words, to the promotion of a viable banking sector. The first stage was characterized by the establishment of a two-tier banking system based on market principles. In this period completely new legal and institutional frameworks had to be established (commercial law, bankruptcy law, accounting standards). Changing macroeconomic environment – price liberalization, devaluation of the currencies, privatization process – also had substantial effects on the financial markets.

The second stage emerged as the period in which a number of mutually interrelated steps, influencing the present and future development of the banking sector, had to be taken. Opening banking sectors to domestic and foreign banks in order to enhance competitiveness, dramatic liberalization of the banking sector. CEECs have been undergoing a complex process of liberalization similar to those in EU countries in the 1970s and 1980s. Setting the basic regulatory and supervisory framework, new operational guidelines and principal for banks' prudential behaviour, the consolidation and re-capitalization of state-owned banks burdened by inherited non-performing loans from centrally planned economies were on the agenda.

The third stage was characterized by the sorting out of problems that accumulated from the previous two stages. Policy-makers have been faced with basic dilemmas in the process of ensuring a viable banking sector. Applied methods of consolidation, re-capitalization and privatization, ways of re-capitalizing or whether to re-capitalize at all before privatization, whom to privatize, sequencing and speed of these steps within the banking sector, were some of the crucial discussion points.

The final stage will be when banking sectors operate on market principles – protective umbrellas are removed – and regulatory and supervisory standards are fully compatible with those in standard market economies. The Czech banking sector has already undergone two stages of its development and is dealing with the third one. However, accomplishing the final stage, i.e. the EU standard, is still far a way.

2 Current stage of the Czech banking system – identification of bottlenecks

The growth of banking institutions and employment in the financial sector accelerated in the period 1990–93. The development reflected the dramatic liberalization of the banking sector including a removal of interest rates ceilings, the openness to newcomers, the improvement of regulatory frameworks, creating new operational guidelines and principal for banks' prudential behaviour. This rapid growth was also pulled by demand factors because of a gap between supply and demand of banking products. However, from 1995 up to now – the third stage – the banking sector finds itself as a whole in difficulties.

2.1 Expansion of the banking sector

As of 1 January 1990 the mono-banking system was replaced by the two-tier banking system. Two commercial banks were carved out from the former Czechoslovak State Bank – Komerční banka in the Czech Republic and Všeobecná úverová banka in the Slovak Republic). In addition, the following banks have already operated: Česká Spořitelna (Savings Bank), Ivnostenská banka, Československá obchodní banka (Czechoslovak Trade Bank) and Investiční a Poštovní banka (former Investtiční banka). Afterwards it was widely accepted that the more banks operating within the financial market, the better; as this would result in the system as a whole being more competitive and efficient.[2]

The rapid growth of new commercial banks in the period 1991–92 brought a certain degree of competition into the financial market but later the financial position of these banks was considerably impaired.

From Table 11.1, one observes the growth of commercial banks in the period 1990–94 and since then their gradual decline.

The Czech Republic (among other countries) had a unique opportunity to start building a banking system almost from scratch. Nevertheless, there are several questions regarding the expansion and openness of the banking system. First, commercial banks were carved out of the former Czechoslovak State Bank (Central Bank). This step was identical for most of the former communist countries undergoing the transformation of domestic banking sectors. But if one looks at the current situation within the segment of the biggest commercial banks it is possible to see different shortcomings in the applied measures. In Poland, nine state-owned regional banks were established instead of one or two large banks. The advantage of such a policy is, at least for the first stage of development, the avoidance of creating 'capture banks'. Decentralization led to covering all major regions in the country and the allocation of credits was better monitored. This might be explained by better knowledge of debtors and regional conditions. On the other hand, experience shows that a regional break-up limits the competitiveness within a given market since banks play dominant position. EBRD, for example, suggests that the break-up of state banks should be organized on the basis of sectoral rather than geographical terms. However, such an organization reduces the advantages of portfolio diversification and increases the probability of a default risk.

Second, this almost 'free entry' of the small and medium sized commercial banks into the banking sector, which was mainly adopted because of the perceived benefits of competition, has been in fact detrimental. Partly unrestrained access has induced a situation where too

Table 11.1　Number of banks in the Czech Republic (as of the end of year)

	1990	1991	1992	1993	1994	1995	1996	1997	1998
Total banks	9	24	37	52	55	54	53	50	47
Big banks	5	6	6	6	6	6	5	5	5
Small banks	4	14	19	22	21	18	12	9	8
Foreign banks	–	4	8	11	12	12	13	14	13
Foreign bank branch offices	–	–	3	7	8	10	9	9	10
Specialized banks	–	–	1	5	7	8	9	9	9
Banks under forced administration	–	–	–	1	1	0	5	4	0

Source: CNB.

many banks serve a limited market. In addition, the newly operating banks were mostly poorly capitalized and managed. At present the growth of operating banks is almost zero – the banking supervision agency stopped giving new banking licences in September 1993 in order to create breathing space for established banks to consolidate their positions.[3]

Third, as for foreign entry the situation is quite different. There is a general consensus that, in the first stage of transition, the activities of foreign banks are neutral in terms of their impact on the banking sector in question. This might be explained by their specific role when these banks mainly provide services to their home country clients who start establishing within the unfolding market economy. Later these banks expand and provide services not only for their home country clients but also for domestic firms and individual clients. For banks from EU countries applying for a banking licence to operate within the Czech system, the CNB should apply slightly different rules. We admit that it is necessary to adopt a strictly selective policy in order to avoid a negative impact on the banking sector from newcomers. But, as noted, the entry of foreign banks has had a positive effect on the domestic banking system for the most part. Hence, if there are some highly regarded foreign banks wishing to operate in the Czech Republic, no obstacles should be imposed by the Czech National Bank. Furthermore, if the CNB continues to apply the restriction policy on foreign banks, this is undoubtedly a negative signal to the European Commission, when subjects wishing to obtain licences do not know what criteria to meet. In other words, this situation can cause doubts as to whether this country will be able to meet one of the essential criteria involved in the 'Second Directive' – to enable a non-domestic credit institution to operate in any member country.

The significant feature of the Czech banking system is a relatively high degree of concentration. This characteristic is not too different compared to developed countries, however, the major Czech banks are well below the standard performance of their peers in these countries. The explanation of the high concentration is also determined, as has already been mentioned, by the adopted policy at the outset of banking reforms. Turning to the data analysis, we can see that these big banks have decisive market shares in assets, deposits and credits (Table 11.2). Looking at the balance sheets of the biggest commercial banks it follows that Česká Spořitelna remains the primary collector of personal deposits and has limited activities in financing corporations. Its lending activities are mainly within the interbank market. Komerčni banka (KB), Investiêni

Table 11.2   Share of banks in total assets (%)

	1993	1994	1995	1996	1997	1998
Large banks	82.3	77.18	71.72	68.87	65.67	68.06
Small banks	8.9	4.44	4.92	5.21	4.72	3.52
Foreign banks incl. Branches	7.2	11.67	16.46	18.84	22.28	22.35
Specialized banks	1.39	1.47	2.11	3.09	4.29	4.04
Banks under conservatorship	0.21	5.24	4.78	4.00	3.04	3.03
Total	100	100	100	100	100	100

Source: CNB

and Poštovní Banka (IPB), and Československá Obchodní Banka (CSOB) show the different structure. These banks are involved primarily in corporate lending. KB and IPB gradually increased their shares in the collection of personal deposits.

The group of small banks differ from the major banks in two basic characteristics: they lacked a more substantial base of primary deposits of their own and were disproportionately engaged in highly risky trades. At the start of their existence, small banks had to build up a branch network from the very beginning and deal with the traditional inclination of depositors who preferred established major banks. Small banks became dependent on central bank refinancing and later on the interbank deposit market. As interest rates on this market were high at the start, these banks concentrated in their assets a high proportion of credits and other claims with a presupposed above average return, which were, however, burdened by a more substantial degree of risk.

2.2   Bad loans the main flaw of the Czech banking system

Despite efforts that have been taking place to cope with problem loans the credit portfolio of commercial banks has continued to be unfavourably affected by a high proportion of problem loans. Though parts of them are still a heritage of the past, an increasing share are the 'new' problem loans, especially but not exclusively, from the initial stage of transition.

There are two basic causes of increasing non-performing loans. Either they arise from adverse local and industrial conditions, or they are a result of a greater propensity of banks to take risk. It is possible to break up the elements of bad loans into two categories: controllable and uncontrollable.

If the major elements of loss loans are controllable it is obvious that banks can avoid losses. First of all, they must improve credit policy – credit analyses, loan structuring etc. A further important aspect of loss prevention is an improvement in management quality. On the other hand, it is very difficult to influence uncontrollable factors since the losses caused by these factors are less predictable. They are conditioned by a number of external factors, which are remarkable, for example, in the agricultural sector.

Identification by banking supervision of the quality of these credits was significantly complicated by the absence of a unified system for the classification of credit portfolios. In 1993 the CNB issued recommendations for this area, but banks respected them only to a certain extent. Only when, in 1994, the CNB issued a crucial provision on the principles of classification of claims on credits and on the creation of reserves and provisions for such credits was it possible to identify poor-quality credits in bank portfolios. This led to substantial growth in recorded classified credits in all problem banks by the end of 1994, when their share in total credits roughly tripled, representing about one-third of the credits in bank portfolios.

The data in Table 11.3 provide identification of trends in the classified client credits of commercial banks in the Czech Republic in the period 1994–98. These banks are also confronted with the corresponding trends in reserves and loan loss provisions. One might observe a gradual decline of total classified loans to total credits. However, this decline should be explained by the fact that the CNB did not include banks under conservatorship.

Parallel to the volume of classified credits; there was also a corresponding decrease in the amount of risk-weighted classified credits, that is, in the amount of reserve requirements. The data indicate that despite the growing volume of reserves and loan-loss provisions, the ratio of actual

Table 11.3 Classified loans (% of total credits)

	1994	1995	1996	1997	1998*
Total classified loans	36.53	33.04	29.33	26.98	27.10
Weighted classification	21.52	20.26	18.82	17.42	17.19
Classified credits adjusted for collateral	n.a.	17.01	14.72	14.55	16.90
Reserve and provisions surplus (+) or shortage (−)	n.a.	−0.28	0.10	−0.03	n.a.

* Excluding Konsolidacni banka and banks under conservatorship.
Source: CNB

to required reserves continued to diminish in the period covered. The trends in both of these ratios suggest that those problem loans and the resulting vulnerability of commercial banks is the highest burden for banks.

2.3   Financial distress –
the group of small and medium sized commercial banks

Identifying the basic cause of the problems of some small banks shows that a rapid credit expansion at the start of their activities was one of them. All banks with solvency problems created the major part of their credit portfolios before the end of 1993. This is particularly obvious with banks that started activity before 1992, where the share of credits recorded in 1993 make up more than 80 per cent of all credits as of the first half of 1996; the highest credit risk exposures also originated in the initial period of their activity. The riskiness of such credits was quite apparent when they came due and debtors were unable to meet their obligations.

An earlier realization of the extent of the problem was not facilitated even by auditors' reports on problem banks – an important factor in verifying the quality of assets and amount of bank losses. With only some exceptions, these reports did not signal any major problems until the end of 1994.

The development of a market mechanism accompanied by vast shifts of property, the development of financial and capital markets, the opening up of borders facilitating substantial migration and other factors associated with the overall economic transformation following 1989, created a hotbed of crime in general, including banking. Along with new banking instruments, schemes of funding and guarantees, new technologies for data transfer and its processing and new business partners, various types and schemes of frauds appeared in banks.

The increase in banking criminal activity was facilitated by the fact that from the beginning, sufficient control mechanisms were not implemented in banks, bank employees lacked experience in new banking transactions and the types of frauds with which they might be confronted and which had already been detected in advanced countries. Also, the weakening of the morals of the people as a heritage of the past regime contributed to the increased criminality.

Legislation stipulating the rights, obligations and scrutiny of participants in the banking market and other financial markets, has been going through significant changes, as has the criminal and legal sphere. Gradually, as know-how is acquired, legal means are being established for a more effective fight against financial criminal activity, including organized crime, concurrent with the restructuring of the police and court systems. The professional level and capacities of the police and courts are not sufficient to investigate and try the larger, more complicated cases.

It can be said that one of the causes of the failures of small Czech banks that have occurred is banking criminality. Many fraudulent financial schemes have been imported to the Czech Republic and successfully implemented in banks. Apart from the most common 'intermediary' frauds, 'transfer' frauds, frauds with letters of credit, cheques, credit cards and computer fraud, the 'primary bank guarantee' – a new type of fraud occurred in the Czech Republic.

3   Methods of banking consolidation and restructuring

The assumption of bad claims from the portfolio of state-owned commercial banks has been the main feature of bank rehabilitation. The great volume of non-performing loans in the portfolio of the state-owned commercial banks is a legacy of the past. In addition, these banks signalled problems of under-capitalization. Cleaning up the bank portfolio from the non-performing credit inherited from the past, solving new problems arising in the banking sector during the transformation process, and a further restructuring of banks in conjunction with their preparation for privatization became the essential steps in this stage. The restructuring, consolidation and stabilization programmes in the banking sector were implemented outside the state budget through the creation of some non-standard, so-called transformation institutions, which were supplied with direct state guarantee for financial resources provision and loss and operating costs coverage. As a result, the indirect potential liabilities of the state in the banking sector emerged.

The bank re-capitalization, consolidation and stabilization programmes were implemented over time in three steps. We will, in the following Sections, discuss only the last two – consolidation and stabilization operations within the small and medium sized commercial banks segment.

3.1   The Consolidation Programme II and Stabilization Programme

The main reason for adopting the measures within Consolidation Programme II was to prevent these problems from weakening the confidence in banking institutions. Though the share of all small sized banks in the bank market was only 9 per cent in 1993, the continuing bankruptcies in this segment of banks gradually undermined public confidence in the banking sector.

Another stimulus for the effort aimed at small bank consolidation was their contribution in the area of client services. In some respects, these banks substantially increased the level of the banking system in the CR. They often offered an individual approach to clients, new products such as home banking, a high-quality and comfortable payment system, short-term investment programmes or current accounts with advantageous interest. They introduced such services either exclusively or quite far ahead of major banks. A banking sector composed only of major banks, where the introduction of each new product means high costs and complex management and banks with exclusive orientation towards large corporate clients would develop slowly and have a lower level of client services.

Moreover, not all small sized banks have had problems and client distrust could also threaten those banks which are, in principle, 'sound'. Since 1994 we have witnessed the failure of several small and medium sized commercial banks. These banks had obtained their financial resources largely via the interbank market, and the biggest banks in the Czech Republic are (were) the main creditors of these small- and medium-sized banks in the market. It is not surprising that the big banks were involved in rescue activities when these events occurred. A particularly prominent role was played by Česká Spořitelna (Savings Bank) and Československá Obchodní Banka (Czechoslovak Trade Bank). Although Česká Spořitelna allegedly lost a huge amount of credits, especially to AB Banka and Bohemia Banka, we cannot trace any sign of systemic risk or rather systemic crises in the banking sector as a whole.

No direct impact of the small and medium sized commercial banks on the Czech-banking system can be traced, since the total assets of these banks amount to 5 per cent of total assets within the banking sector. Nevertheless, the decline of small-sized banks cannot be neglected, since it could cause not only systemic risk (crisis) in this segment of the banking sector, but also the decline of confidence in the banking sector.

Even if the likelihood of failure of some commercial banks in the Czech Republic is still possible, we would not envisage that the decline of small banks could lead to an epidemic in the banking system as a whole. This is, of course, a matter of *ad hoc* judgement, the reason for this assumption lies in the 'too big to fail', or rather, 'too important to fail' doctrine. These 'big' banks are too important in the Czech banking system; we presume that they have such a strong foothold that they are able to deal with whatever disturbances there may be within the banking system. In fact, the state is a shareholder in these banks and thus the government will support these big banks if a solvency problem arises, for example Česká Spořitelna.

The main weaknesses, excluding those where financial crime was present, of the small- and medium-sized banks can be identified as follows:

- Insufficient capital;
- The lack of primary deposits;
- Inappropriate assets–liabilities mismatch;
- No transparency of shareholders;
- A problem of adverse selection due to relatively high interest rates;
- Inadequate management in many cases.

A glance at the above problems supports the idea that one of the possible ways of resolving the problems would be a merger of the small banks with bigger, healthier banks. However, we argue that this solution has not been widely adopted in the Czech-banking sector. Reasons to be sceptical can also be found in the experience in other countries. First of all, it is desirable to analyse the benefits of mergers among banks. The following are very often quoted as key causes leading to mergers:

- an effort by banks to become a member of a core bank group;
- to secure unrealized economies of scale;
- to carry out the rationalization of branch networks;
- to enable the demands of large customers to be met;
- to match the size of other banks in international banking;
- to meet foreign bank competition on their home ground.

Applying these factors to the Czech-banking sector, there is minimal incentive for mergers or take-overs by domestic banks. The same situation can be seen in mergers of foreign commercial banks. We observe that there is absolutely no incentive to be active in these operations. One possible explanation is that the advantages are not significant, at most marginal. The small banks mentioned have a few or no branches and their clients are mainly small private companies, which are not good performers. The process of mergers and acquisition in the Czech Republic can be seen from Table II in the Appendix.

Nevertheless, one way of how to proceed might be to eliminate undesirable banks by increasing the minimum capital requirement for banks – a measure, which would have a relatively fast and positive impact on the banking structure. Above all, it is desirable to emphasize the measure prior to taking this step; there is a need to make clear which size banks, in terms of capital levels, should be 'eliminated'. Unfortunately, the secondary consequence of this step is that a few of the small banks that do not have any difficulties at present would also have to either increase their capital or merge with a larger bank.

An indirect way of increasing capital was applied in the Czech banking system. Since a number of small-sized banks have a great volume of bad loans, the CNB decided, within the framework of a consolidation programme, to oblige these banks to increase their capital in order to cover their bad loans. If they are not able to do so, the CNB will put these banks under forced (special) administration and look for a strategic partner. If no other investor can be found relatively quickly, Konsolidacni banka temporarily takes over the bank. It is worth noting, that the above mentioned method, i.e., forced administration, is an operation often used as a temporary solution for failed banks. During this period the authority seeks bridge banks, new banks or other institutions which will ensure the stability of the bank in question. These operations have a positive effect, in the sense of avoiding a further deterioration in the financial position of the bank in question. Such a method was, for example, applied when Barings failed in 1995. The bank was under the administration of the Bank of England and then sold to ING, the Dutch banking and insurance group (see Lastra, 1996).

The last, but not necessarily least, way of dealing with failed institutions is to revoke the banking licence of the bank in question. Such a step avoids further deterioration of the situation. On the other hand, it should be said that this step could have negative consequences as far as the credibility of the banking sector is concerned. In addition this solution can be costly. Therefore, any hasty decision on the part of the banking supervisory body or other authorities could be very harmful. But when a bank has failed owing to fraud, liquidation is the appropriate response.

3.2   The ways of rescuing activities in the banking sector

Undoubtedly, all the above methods of sorting out the troubled institutions are costly. The CNB decided to run a so-called Consolidation programme II and later the government announced a further programme helping medium- and small-sized commercial banks – Stabilization programme.

Consolidation Programme II, was implemented by the CNB at the end of 1995 and beginning of 1996 and focused on the small- and medium-sized banks. The objective of the stabilization programme was to solve the remaining problem in the banks through injections of additional private capital and recapitalization through profit generation.

Ceska Financni (Czech Financial Corporation, Ltd., (CF)), was created as a CNB subsidiary in February 1997. The corporation was created for the purpose of implementing the consolidation and stabilization programmes and to administer the CNB non-performing credits and property participation taken from small banks. The stabilization programme began in 1996 and it is planned to finish in 2003, when all the losses and assets write-offs will be compensated from the National Property Fund to the Consolidation Bank. Since privatization is almost complete and its income is expected to be low, there is some doubt that NPF will be able to compensate the stabilization programme at termination. Therefore, there exists some probability that the costs would have to be covered by government. Moreover, Consolidation Bank has issued its own bonds to finance the stabilization program for small and medium banks, consequently there maybe be additional costs transferred to the state. The consolidation program administered by the CF is financed from the CNB compensations.

In the framework of the bank stabilization programme where 6 banks participated, the CF bought CZK 10.633 billion assets in nominal value from which CZK 7.536 were loans and CZK 3.097 were shares. In addition in 1997 CF bought assets in the framework of the consolidation programme for small- and medium-size banks in the amount CZK 11.466 billion from which credits were CZK 8.369 billion and the rest CZK 3.097 were shares. Moreover, CF conducted the activities of the banks that had had their licences revoked. The CF is financed from CNB and Consolidation Bank. In 1997 CNB provided CZK 9.638 billion in 17.5 per cent interest and KOB CZK 12.3 in lower interest rate related to the PRIBOR rate.

In February 1998, the government decided to increase CF financing by CZK 5 billion. In April 1998, CF transferred CZK 9 billion as capital injection to Agrobanka (AGB). The total amount cash transfer from CNB to the CF to buy the AGB assets during 1998 was CZK 22 billion. By the end of 1997 the amount of CZK 17.499 billion (71 per cent) of the CF total assets (CZK 24.6 billion) were in overdue payment from 30 days to 1 year (35 per cent of total assets more than a year overdue). Only CZK 0.23 billion, about 1 per cent of the total assets were (realized) paid during the year from which 0.9 per cent were from the consolidation programme assets.

The government, through the Czech Financial Corporation Ltd, a special institution set up for this purpose as a subsidiary of the CNB, temporarily purchased the bad assets at face value, up to 110 per cent of respective bank capital. The bought assets return had to be bought back within a period of 5 to 7 years. The banks did not have to pay interest. The programme was initially financed through the extension of short-term credit from the CNB to Czech Financial Corporation Ltd. Further, the CF was refinanced at market cost through the Consolidation Bank that issued bonds for this purpose. The CNB also extended credit to CF together with the transfer of bad assets bought by the central bank during the second stage of consolidation programme. Thus, following the restructuring, consolidation and stabilization of the banking sector analysed above the Czech government ended up with a high implicit fiscal exposure in the banking sector.

The Bank also began to participate in consortium loans in co-operation with large financial institutions. The loans granted by the KOB were based on the bank policy and the government's decision for restructuring and revitalization programmes for some enterprises such as Aero, the aviation holding company and revitalization of Ekoagrabanka. Following the government decision the KOB is associated with a programme for consolidating the stability of the banking sector adopted at the end of 1996. KOB, using sources provided by National Property Fund, granted a loan to Czech Financial Corporation Ltd of CZK 12.3 billion to refinance the risky assets purchased from banks

4   The cost and effects
of the consolidation and stabilization programmes

During the stabilization programme of small and medium size banks the Czech National Bank also took over claims and participation shares of the problem banks included in the programme. The government through the NPF issued a guarantee to the CNB that covers the losses accrued over the stabilization programme. If the state was to take over the claims and losses of the CNB it would have to increase the government debt and budget deficit by a significant amount.

The method used to rescue Ekoagrobanka was employed as a model. This approach, quite common in standard economies, was an illustration of rapid intervention. Its use was only made possible by an amendment to the Act on the CNB allowing a capital decrease of a problem bank. Thereby, scope was created for the bank's take-over by another investor without having to negotiate the purchase of actually worthless shares from former shareholders. In future possible rescues of problem banks, it will be necessary to prevent shareholders, if a bank has financial problems, from calculating on a capital decrease as an acceptable recourse, which will not be of great danger to the main shareholders. For this reason, this approach has to be applied relatively early.

A specific problem is the absence of any institution which would – with state support, common in similar situations abroad – participate in the rescue of threatened banks. If no private sector entity is interested, such an institution would enter into banks, salvage and sell them. This method is not only cleaner from the system point of view, but usually also cheaper. To date, negotiations with 'state institutions' (KOB, Èeská inkasní) about such activity have been unsuccessful.

Another, similar problem is the lack of a mechanism for purchasing less sound assets prior to the commencement of potential problems. The CNB has already prepared a model for a centralized solution of bad debt problems with possible state support. This model presupposes the establishment of a unit for the purchase and management of non-performing bank assets, whose founders might be the CNB and the MF, with perhaps the participation of IFC (International Financial Corporation).

This unit would, based on bank requirements, purchase their bad debts, or possibly other assets, for which it would pay in cash an est-imated sum. The remaining value (possibly decreased by 10 to 20 per cent) would be transferred to a subordinated debt of the unit towards a bank. This method would also enable a certain degree of state support of such operations to a precisely determined volume (strengthening of the credit of a subordinated debt, the purchase of a certain part of non-performing assets for higher than the market price etc.).

The banking sector development described above is also associated with the fact that in recent years the state incurred substantial expenses connected to banking sector stabilization. These included operations directed at the banks' clearing of assets linked with the pre-transforma-tion economy and those connected to the transformation.

In the first case, these were expenses of Consolidation Programme I, generated by the transfer of revolving credits on inventories into KOB, re-capitalization of banks from NPF funds and the rescue of CSOB's balance through CE. The total amount of expenses on these operations will be known after all credit cases have been concluded, after the repayment or writing off of credits granted. At present, the preliminary CNB estimate of these expenses is about CZK 60 bn.

Table 11.4 The assessment of the costs for banks' consolidation and stabilization (CZK billion)

Type of programme	Type of expenses	costs
Consolidation Programme I	Establishing KOB	6
	Reserves for KOB	31
	Transfering debts from state-owned banks	22
	Lost of KOB	14–15
	Compensation of the losses in 96	5.1
	Transfer of assets from CSOB to CF	20
	Estimation of losses from Slovak Encashment	10
Consolidation Programme II	Financial support of the small- and medium-sized banks	40.3
	Loss of AGB	12–20
Stabilization Programme	Interest compensation*	2.5
Total		160.9–171.9

*Costs for the first two years of programme. In seven years costs are estimated to be CZK 16 mld.

Source: Hospodarske noviny

As regards banking sector problems originating during the transformation stage, the first expenses arose in connection with Kreditní a prumyslová banka, AB banka and Bank Bohemia. In 1996, the consolidation process continued via steps described in the previous section. Other potential expenses arose, generally divided into the following groups:

- Expenses for deposit compensation above the Deposit Insurance Scheme limit in Prvni slezska banka, Podnikatelska banka, Velkomoravska banka and Realitbanka. These are not cases of net losses, as the expenses will have to be decreased by the share from sales of assets. In some cases, the CNB opted for support by a take-over of a problem bank by a sound bank. In addition to reducing banking sector destabilization in the public mind, this solution also has comparatively lower costs. Support was procured for take-overs of the following banks: COOP banka, Bankovni dum Skala, Ekoagrobanka and Evrobanka.
- Reduction of economic effects on the banking sector resulting from some bank bankruptcies. In this case, support was provided to those banks suffering mostly from the fact that banks going bankrupt were unable to meet commitments to them.

These operations, carried out from 1994, have involved about CZK 30 bn. In this case also, we cannot determine the precise amount. The expenses will depend on the efficiency of the administration of both acquired and residual assets. As regards assets administered by the CNB, a specialized team was created to achieve maximum revenues.

5 Conclusion

Experience shows that no banking sector is secure beforehand against the possibility of problems emerging in individual banks or their groups, or even against bank crises on a small or large scale. Bank crises are frequent even in advanced market economies. It is thought that the main reason lies with the discrepancy between the rapidity and extent of financial operations on one hand and the degree of flexibility and adaptability of the real economy on the other. Moreover, a new dimension is emerging, the ongoing globalization in the conditions of an information society. This is why the main target in this area is the prevention of system crisis at both national and international levels. This orientation should also include the creation of cushions 'bumpers', special funds, whose usage would stop an emerging crisis or at least moderate its extent.

Thus, the risk to the development of the Czech banking sector involves this generally valid component, multiplied, moreover, by the specific domestic position. This position originates not only in the character of the economic transformation, but also in the still inadequate regulation of the environment in which banks operate. We have in mind both the earlier mentioned legislative problems, but mainly the character and composition of the domestic financial market, where banks are undoubtedly the most strictly regulated entities. However, they are affected by the consequences of the inefficient regulation of other parts of the financial market (capital in particular). For example, the present 'struggle for majorities' can potentially weaken the financial strength of banks and decrease their credibility.

Obviously, the development of Czech banks is proceeding very quickly and their financial force and know-how are currently at an incomparably higher level than several years ago. Nevertheless, it is necessary to take into account that in the Czech banking sector, even the strongest and soundest banks are in international terms only banks which 'are not too unsound'. Domestic banks still have to take many steps to approach the level of banks in most advanced countries.

The elimination of insolvent banks does not guarantee survival of other banks. If people are uncertain, as is the case now, even comparatively good banks are exposed to the risk of liquidity crises, which can easily be generated even by completely unjustified information. In the next stage also, bank activities will be exposed to the above-average risky environment of the Czech economy, and to increasing competition on the bank market, which is suppressing interest margins. They will also be affected by the ongoing regulation of other parts of the financial system and by the not quite adequate legal infrastructure.

An analysis of the banking sector, its development, present position and the measures directed at its consolidation, makes it possible to identify the causes of its problems. The analysis shows, that in addition to limitations in the banking sector itself and its relationships to subjects in the real economy sector, there are causes of a more general nature related to the overall financial sector and its institutions; besides banks, investment funds and companies in particular, as well as capital market institutions, insurance companies and pension funds, and the legislative and institutional framework within which both financial and non-financial sectors operate.

The main limitation of the current position consists in the fact that the processes of changing the legislative and system framework, of forming financial market institutions and enforcing consistent observance of contracts and 'rules of the game' of a market economy lagged far behind the growth of the financial sector, increased by the weight and branches of its subjects as well as by the diversification and sophistication of its products. Liberalization of the financial markets, and also their increasing technological level, calls for a correlative adjustment of legislation and of controlling and regulatory institutions.

Notes

1 The views and opinions expressed in this study are those of the authors and are not necessarily those of the Czech National Bank.
2 The argument widely used by the private sector was based on the false idea that foreign banks could strengthen competitive pressures within the banking sector. There has been no evidence in EU countries that foreign banks have substantially influenced competitive pressures on domestic banks.
3 Three foreign banks obtained licences from the CNB – Midland Bank, Westdeutsche Landesbank and GE Capital Bank (the banking licence of Westdeutsche Landesbank was revoked since the bank did not start operations).

References

Begg, D. and Portes, R. (1992) Enterprise Debt and Economic Transformation in Central and Eastern Europe, *CEPR Discussion Paper*, 695.

Benston, G. J. (1985) An Analysis of the Causes of Savings and Loans Association Failures, *Monograph Series in Finance and Economics*, New York: University/ Blackwell.

Caprio, G. and Klingebiel, D. (1996) Bank Insolvency: Bad Luck, Bad Policy, or Bad Banking?, paper prepared for the World Bank's Annual Bank Conference on Development Economics, Washington, DC, 25–26 April.

Cole, D. W. (1972) A Return-on-Equity Model for Banks, *The Bankers Magazine*, Summer, p. 1–15.

Dewatripont, M. and Tirole, J. (1993) *The Prudential Regulation of Banks*, London: MIT Press.

Foster, G. (1986) *Financial Statement Analysis*, 2nd edn, New Jersey: Prentice-Hall.

Freixas, X. and Rochet, J. C. (1997) *Microeconomics of Banking*, Cambridge: MIT Press.

Fry, M. (1988) *Money, Interest and Banking in Economic Development*, Baltimore, MD: The Johns Hopkins University Press.

Gilbert, R. A. (1991) Market Discipline and Bank Risk: Theory and Evidence, *Federal Reserve Bank of St Louis Review*, 72, 1–18.

Gorton, G. (1984) Banking Panics and Business Cycles, *Oxford Economics Papers*, no. 40.

Hellwig, M. (1991) Banking, Financial Intermediation and Corporate Finance, in A. Giovanni and C. Mayer (eds), *European Financial Integration*, Cambridge: Cambridge University Press.

Hrnčíř, M. (1992) Money and Credit in the Transition of the Czechoslovak Economy, in H. Siebert (ed.), *The Transformation of Socialist Economies*, Kiel: Kiel Symposium.

Chew, D. (ed., 1991) *New Developments in Commercial Banking*, Oxford: Basil Blackwell.

Lastra, R. M. (1996) 'Central Banking and Banking Regulation', Financial Market Group, London: London School of Economics.

Mejstrík, M. (1997) The Emergence of Institutional Owners: The role of Banks and Nonbanking Financial Institutions in the Privatization of the Economy and the Banks, in M. Mejstøík (ed.), *The Privatization Process in East-Central Europe. Evolutionary Process of Czech Privatizations*, Dordrecht-Boston-London: Kluwer Academic Publishers.

Mullineaux, A. W. (1993) *Privatisation and Banking Sector Reform: Lessons from Poland*, The University of Birmingham, Department of Economics, Discussion Paper.

Appendix

Table 11.1   Small banks under liquidation, conservatorship and prepared for mergers

Name of bank	Operational start date	CNB administration	Liquidation	Method
Agrobanka	01–07–90	17–09–96	08–10–98	Take-over by GE
AB Banka	01–04–91	–	05–03–96	Licence revocation (15–12–96)
Banka Bohemia	29–01–91	31–03–94	18–07–94	Licence revocation (18–07–94)
Bankovni dum Skala	13–12–90	–	10–12–97 to 30–04–98	Take-over by Union banka, licence revocation (31–03–97)
COOP banka	24–2–92	23–04–96	–	Take-over by Foresbanka Licence revocation
Ceska banka	15–01–92	–	19–03–96 to 27–06–96	Licence revocation (15–12–95), Bankruptcy (28–06–1996)
Ekoagrobanka	01–11–90	16–01–96	01–01–98	Take-over by Union banka, licence revocation (31–05–97)
Evrobanka	01–10–91	–	–	Take-over by Union banka, licence revocation (30–06–97)
Kreditni a prumyslova banka	01–10–91	30–09–93 to 31–08–95	–	Licence revocation, (02–10–95), Bankruptcy (02–10–95)
Kreditni banka Plzen	01–01–90	–	01–10–96	Licence revocation (08–08–96),
Podnikatelska banka	18–12–92	06–06–96	–	n.a.
Prvni slezska banka	12–01–93	–	24–07–96	Licence revocation (13–05–96) Bankruptcy (20–11–97)
Realitbanka	01–11–91	10–07–96	–	Licence revocation (17–04–97), Bankruptcy (24–03–97)
Velkomoravska	03–11–92	10–07–96	–	Licence revocation 24–10–98 Bankruptcy 02–07–96
Pragobanka	01–10–90			Licence revocation 24–10–98 Bankruptcy 19–11–98
Universal bank	12–02–93			Licence revocation (10–02–1999) Bankruptcy (12–02–99)

Source: CNB.

Table 11.II Costs of consolidation programme

Bank	Costs of Consolidation (CZK bil.)	Paid by
Agrobanka	n.a.	CNB
AB Banka	2.8	CNB
Banka Bohemia	11.7	CNB
Bankovní dùm Skala	3.18	CNB
COOP banka	1.2	CNB
Ceska banka	n.a.	
Ekoagrobanka	9.0	CNB
Evrobanka	8.9	CNB
Kreditni a prùmyslova banka	0.6	CNB
Kreditni banka Plzen	n.a.	
Podnikatelska banka	1.24	CNB
První slezska banka	0.2	CNB
Realitbanka	0.2	CNB
Velkomoravska banka	1.15	CNB
Pragobanka	n.a.	
Universal bank	n.a.	

Source: Ministry of Finance.

V
Hungary

12
Turbulences and Emergency Landings in Leased Planes: Macroeconomic Stabilization and Financial Sector Reform in Hungary in the 1990s

Ádám Török

The title of this chapter refers to quite special aeroplanes existing probably only in our imagination: they have been permanently exposed to harsh weather and conditions that their crews have not always been entirely familiar with, their technology was outdated, they were mainly in their last years of service and, in addition to all the flight related problems outlined, the financial background of the flights was far from stable most of the time. Still, the airline company using these planes has been able to survive despite all these problems. It did not become a major market player, but it has never given up service and is probably considered not an upmarket airline, but a modest and reliable firm anyway.

The aeroplane example refers to the Hungarian financial sector, and the airline in question may be understood as the Hungarian economy. Twenty years ago IMF membership seemed still unthinkable (and far more so Hungarian participation in European integration), and less than ten years have passed since the highly unstable financial sector of this country was still considered a kind of time bomb with its indebted state-owned banks, very underdeveloped capital market and almost astronomical gross foreign debt.

The latest EU Commission assessment of the candidate countries published in November 1998 praised Hungary as the best performer in economic transition, including the financial part of the process.[1] What happened in the meantime?

This chapter is not meant to give an overall assessment of the transition in the Hungarian financial sector. Rather, it is focusing on turbulences in the financial sector as we understand them, including 'emergency landings' when the government had to intervene drastically in order to prevent the country's financial sector from becoming a loose cannon. Our concept of Hungarian financial sector development during the last 20 years, but above all in the last 10 years is one of a more or less continuous sequence of crisis situations appearing in different dimensions (foreign debt, domestic banking, domestic budget, domestic capital markets etc.).

Solutions provided to these crises proved more or less durable and defendable in debates with the economics profession, but most of them helped financial sector transition as well as its role in crisis management. With some exaggeration, emergency-related actions by the government and/or the central bank were at least as effective in developing the financial sector of the country as any kind of existing or only virtual strategy of transition in this sector.

The chapter consists of four parts. Part 1 gives an overview of financial developments in Hungary related, of course, to the overall transition process. Part 2 comes up with a short assessment of macroeconomic policies with impacts on the financial sector. Part 3 offers institutional analysis with special emphasis on the banking sector. Part 4 summarizes and concludes.

1   Hungarian financial and macro-developments in the 1990s

Hungary's long, but quite cautious pre-1990 reform efforts had two major elements concerning the financial sector. One of these was crucial for financing the country's towering gross foreign debt,[2] which had surpassed USD 10 billion by 1982, the year of Hungary's admission to the IMF and the World Bank.

Hungary had first asked for Soviet political approval for joining these international financial institutions back in 1967 (Antalóczy, 1996). This approval was only granted 15 years later. The main argument accepted was not the one of Romanian membership since 1972 (and, a fact not mentioned by the author referred to: Vietnam was also a member due to its takeover of South Vietnam's membership at the annexion of the latter in 1975). The Soviets had to admit that they became unable to co-finance Hungary's programme of financial stabilization and debt reduction. The Soviet Union had to suffer considerable financial losses owing to the fact that it could not benefit very much from oil price increases because most of its exports went to Eastern Europe on a clearing basis. On the other hand, Hungary's external finances became even more fragile in 1982 as a result of the then debt crisis of Latin America.

The second major reform step in the financial sector took place in 1987. The previously existing two-tier banking system was then re-established. The main goal of this banking reform was promoting competition between banks and creating an effective commercial banking sector able to deal with companies without any government intervention (Surányi, 1998). In the one-tier banking system, the National Bank of Hungary was both a central bank and the country's *de facto* only commercial bank supplying companies with credits.

The 1987 banking reform consisted of creating three new commercial banks out of three major sectoral and regional departments of the National Bank of Hungary. Besides these three new banks, the two other banks formerly (and rather formally) independent from the National Bank of Hungary also became fully chartered financial institutions. These two were the Hungarian Foreign Trade Bank Ltd. and OTP, the country's quasi monopolist savings and loan institution. OTP subsequently became the country's leading retail bank.

Banking reform represented a very important, but still quite formal step towards effective financial sector reform. In fact, it did not have any visible impact on the macro-financial performance of the economy. Figures 12.1 to 12.3 show the extent of financial crises and/or turbulences of the Hungarian economy during the last decade. We are going to assess major trends in GDP growth, foreign debt, balance of payments, inflation and the budget deficit skipping possible arguments on how to define the 'macrofinancial performance' of an economy and the monetary and fiscal components of this somewhat vague term.

The rate of inflation measured by CPI has never been below 10 per cent since 1987, and growth had an almost one-decade long time period of stagnation.[3] Government efforts toward accelerating growth without genuine structural changes both on the supply side and in the financial sector failed several times in such a way that the increment of domestic demand generated by these efforts pulled imports rather than domestic production. Cycles representing the macroeconomic indicators shown above on the one hand and 'macrofinancial' indicators such as gross foreign debt, current account balance and fiscal deficit on the other might help explain the damage caused by irresponsible or simply too optimistic growth policies.

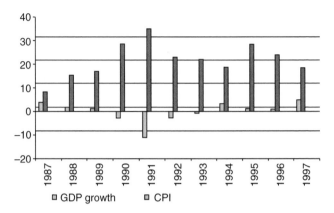

Figure 12.1   Annual GDP growth (constant prices) and consumer prices index, both in percentage

Source: NBH Annual Report 1997. pp. 198, 234.

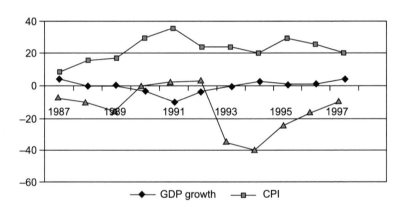

Figure 12.2   Annual GDP growth (constant prices) and consumer prices index, both in percentage – trends compared with current account position (latter shown on a scale of USD 100 million for better comparability)

Source: NBH Annual Report 1997. pp. 198, 234, 254–257.

Figure 12.2 relates current account deficit to cyclical changes in growth and inflation. First, we will briefly discuss fiscal deficit and then turn to foreign debt.

The simplified cyclical trends show quite well that prior to the shock therapy of 1995 the rate of inflation could be diminished and current

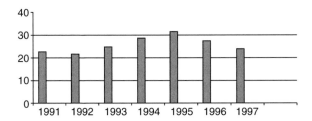

Figure 12.3 Hungary's gross foreign debt including intercompany loans 1990–97 (USD billion)
Source: NBH Annual Report 1997. p. 277.

account temporarily consolidated only if growth was slowed down. This was extremely visible in the early 1990s.

This problem can be put in the framework of an international comparison which makes it clear that Hungary's relatively fast-track approach to economic reform in the early 1990s together with its persisting and deep structural problems made the economy vulnerableto current account variations. Hungary was the first central European country that experienced serious problems with current account sustainability (Krzak, 1998, p. 32). According to Krzak, these problems started in 1993 but became acute in late 1994 and early 1995.

We would slightly disagree with this judgment owing to the fact that the current account deteriorated parallel with the acceleration of growth – exactly from 1993 – but Krzak is right in making it plain that current account deficit became dramatic for the economy as part of a *twin deficit* problem. Budget deficit was above 5 per cent of GDP for a number of years beginning with 1992 whereas current account deficit remained above 9 per cent of GDP in 1993 and 1994.

This twin deficit caused an upsurge in gross foreign debt. To put it in a simple way, Hungary's gross foreign debt:

- surpassed the USD 10 billion limit in 1978 as a result of the country's *poor reaction to the oil crisis* (increased energy bill financed basically from borrowing abroad);[4]
- went over the 20 billion limit in 1986 and 1987 due to the government's *miscalculated growth acceleration effort* meant to replace (or prevent) reform; and
- increased to over USD 30 billion by 1995 owing to the *third aggressive growth effort* in 20 years.

Figure 12.3 shows the development of Hungary's gross foreign debt between 1990 and 1997. The graph depicts two clearly distinct time periods: the first one can be characterized as 'reform with debt increase' and the second as 'reform with debt decrease'. In our opinion, financial sector reform and, in a more narrow approach, banking reform is a major factor underlying and possibly explaining the difference between these two successive time periods.

Hungary's case would be a good example to show that economic reform and macroeconomic stabilization are very far from being mutually inclusive, at least in a transition economy. Hungary was leading the pack of Central East European reform countries after 1980,[5] but it belonged to the worst performers of CEECs both in terms of growth and macroeconomic balances.[6]

All governments from 1987, that is including the last Communist ones were sincerely for economic reforms (or for promoting the transition process), but their ability to combine reform with stabilization or at least effective macroeconomic management was limited. These limits were due, in part, to the debt pressure on the economy which, as opposed to the Czech experience, was a major constraint on Hungarian economic policy since 'the disruptive effect of a potential default has been regarded too costly by policy-makers' (Urban, 1998, p. 31).

Regardless of the policy constraints, an element of Hungarian government philosophy[7] also deserves mention. This element goes back to the central role of public law quite crucial in Hungarian political *cum* legal opposition to the Habsburgs between the sixteenth and the nineteenth century. Legal considerations instead of macro-management related or economic ones had been a key factor in shaping policy decisions before World War II, and this approach was brought back by József Antall, the Prime Minister after the first free elections of 1990.

Without any attempt to simplify Antall's approach to government, his focus was on creating the appropriate legal framework of democracy and market economy. The underlying idea seemed to be that a good legal framework would be instrumental in creating effective government, and this would, in turn, strongly help the administration design effective economic policies. Antall's government achieved very much in privatization and creating modern laws on competition, banking, bankruptcy, human resources management, foreign trade and many other fields, but the economy's macro level performance declined during the last part of his lifetime.[8]

Effective aggregate demand management and shock therapy resulting thereafter in quite fast macro-level stabilization were undertaken only by the next government, a Socialist-Liberal coalition taking office after the elections in May 1994. The shock therapy named after Minister of Finance Lajos Bokros took effect in March 1995. This package included:

- a one-time currency devaluation of 9 per cent;
- the introduction of a temporary import surcharge of 8 per cent;
- the announcement of a crawling peg system of continuous but pre-determined devaluation; and
- considerable cuts in social and general government spending.

The favourable macro-economic impacts of the package were briefly shown in the figures above. Our focus is rather on the changes in macroeconomic policies influencing the financial sector.

2   Macroeconomic policies and the financial sector

It has been pointed that external debt was the key factor determining Hungarian economic policy efforts from the mid-1980s until about 1996, while the role of legal considerations was strong in promoting institutional and economic reforms. Still, the second set of considerations seemed to prevail in the first half of the nineties. It is quite telling that the huge amount of legal changes was accompanied by soaring public debt: the ratio *net consolidated public debt/GDP* increased from 43.9 to 63.2 per cent between 1991 and 1994.

This was mainly due to the so-called debt spiral: high real interest rates together with low growth led to debt explosion (Barabás, Hanecz and Neményi, 1998, p. 790). This seemed unavoidable in the given policy framework because the government considered high real interest rates a necessity for maintaining savings propensity at the level deemed essential for servicing public debt.[9] This policy was, in fact and as one of its critics said 'selling out real stability in the future for apparent stability at present', but it has to be seen that the government had no real choice in the given structural framework. The structure of government spending was so inefficient that revenues from privatization were also spent on current expenditure.

Immediate and profound structural changes were needed because high real interest rates were sending interest rates themselves upwards parallel with public debt (Barabás *et al.*, 1998, p. 790). The main reason was the *crowding-out* effect. Savings were attracted by low-risk and high-yield government bonds which created a shortage of supply on the capital market. This shortage of supply of capital available to the corporate sector drove interest rates still higher on the capital market. In order to remain competitive on the demand side of this market, the government had to enter the interest race or, as referred to in the note to the paragraph above, it had to offer unusually favourable fiscal incentives to investors.

Moreover, *seigniorage* was losing its importance owing to decreasing inflation after 1991 and to the National Bank's policy of paying interest on obligatory reserves of commercial banks. This latter policy might have been understandable as an incentive pushing the banking sector towards higher accumulation. Still, it seems to us that economic liberalization should not necessarily comprise such central bank policy tools which are essential for maintaining monetary and fiscal stability.

Several sources tell us that another reason for abnormally high real interest rates were excessive margins of banks in Eastern Europe in general, but certainly in Hungary.[10] The low efficiency of banks was substantiated by their dispersed network of points of service, the low average level of exposure of clients (first of all households in retail banking) to their banks, the quite great number of households and potential corporate clients outside the reach of the banking sector and, last but not least, their obsolete infrastructure and oversize but undertrained staff. Costs of this inefficiency had to be paid by those rare corporate clients which were deemed creditworthy by the client rating units of the commercial banks.[11] Credit rating activities performed by banks themselves due to the lack of specialized agencies to that effect is a telling sign of the dispersed and vastly inefficient character of the Hungarian financial sector prior to 1995.

Hungarian commercial banks, used to comfortable oligopolies and astronomical profits in the years 1987–90 (Szelényi and Ursprung, 1998, p. 8) had to get accustomed to increasingly bumpy rides from 1990 on. While the years of their apparent success could be regarded as a justification for the creation of the two-tier banking system in 1987, the post-1990 period made it clear that the unfolding of the market economy would make it necessary to continue banking sector reform. The burden of the so-called bad debts became important from 1992 with the wave of corporate bankruptcies, but the underlying reasons for the bankruptcies included the collapse of the Soviet market, the persisting growth crisis and losses of domestic market shares by an array of Hungarian companies due to sweeping import liberalization between 1989 and 1991.[12]

It is worthwhile quoting Surányi (1998, p. 1) at this point: 'bad debts were not only inherited from the past – in which case the whole issue would be merely a stock problem – but they were generated by the banks themselves as well which is clearly a flow problem.' This assessment makes plain the *dynamic* character of the problem of the state-owend banks in Hungary. In fact, these banks had been launched with partly low-quality portfolios, but the quality of these portfolios deteriorated further while these banks still seemed to flourish.

Government action seemed more and more justified and urgent in order to stabilize the banking sector which, to use air traffic parlance borrowed for the title of this paper, became increasingly similar to a plane that had left its normal route and was facing an increasing probability that a costly emergency landing was the only means to avoid crashing. The difference between the situation described in the title and the one analysed here is that the in-flight danger facing Hungarian banks 'modelled' as aeroplanes did not arise from air turbulence, but rather as a combined result of an array of technical problems:

- *obsolete mechanical structures* (the lack of organizational reforms within the banks);
- *a bad fuel-performance relationship at the engine level* (banks were seemingly profitable, but the real long-term cost of this apparent profitability was far too high);[13]
- *incorrect flight plans* (banks' strategies were not in conformity with their economic environment, first of all with the real condition of many Hungarian enterprises);
- *crew related problems* (banks were overstaffed but had only few employees trained to modern banking requirements).

It is perhaps the most dramatic part of our analogy that the in-flight problems outlined above were not detected before takeoff. Or if and when they were, ground staff may have thought the costs of repair and delay would be far too high compared to the risks of any unexpected in-flight event.

Our analogy can be expanded towards the regulatory framework of banking. It is documented by Surányi (1998, pp. 3–4) that the Hungarian government made efforts towards improving the legal environment of the financial sector. This package of measures implemented in 1991 is called 'legislative shock therapy' by Surányi, and it took place quite some time before the consolidation of the banks or their subsequent privatization. These measures can be understood as amendments in flight regulations which cannot replace technical and/or organizational solutions to the problems outlined above. Still, they can make flying somewhat less risky and less costly for airlines unable to solve those problems on their own.

These legal changes went much beyond the banking sector. They were meant, in the first place, to help stabilize the economy without implementing shock therapy in economic policy.[14] The package consisted of three major elements:[15]

- The Banking Act (Act LXIX of 1991 on Financial institutions and financial activities) became effective in December 1991. This piece of legislation required banks to accumulate loan loss provisions. *It made prudential regulation an integral part of Hungarian banking regulation.* Other elements of prudential regulation included the requirement of capital adequacy ratios of 8 per cent set as a target to be reached obligatorily by banks by January 1994, and limits were put on large credits and connected lending. The Banking Act followed, in general, BIS accords although it allowed for some partial solutions made necessary by local conditions or ones linked to the transition process.

  The regulation did not explicitly allow universal banking, but commercial banks gained freedom in running their own subsidiaries trading in securities and running investment funds. In our opinion, the latter quite liberal measure was meant to help establish a wide network of such securities firms in Hungary which would have strong capital bases thanks to their mother banks.[16]
- The Act on Accounting (XVIII/1991) which created conformity between Hungarian accounting standards and the IAS (International Accounting Standards). This law became effective as of 1 January 1992. One of the most important consequences of its implementation was a widespread re-assessment of the quality of the assets and of the economic performance of Hungarian firms. A major element of changes introduced by this law consisted in that it made the 'cashflow' principle prevail: it only allowed registration of such revenues by firms as were really transferred to their bank accounts.
- The Bankruptcy Act (Act IL of 1991 on Bankruptcy, liquidation and final settlements) came into effect in April 1992. It contained very strict rules of bankruptcies and receivership. Although it generated shock waves of enterprise liquidations, it was thereafter widely regarded as an effective measure towards restoring financial discipline in the Hungarian economy.

The 'legislative shock therapy' had dramatic impacts on the Hungarian banking sector, and it weakened banks further instead of stabilizing them. It turned out that most commercial banks were unable to collect loan loss provisions required by this law, and the number of banks proving able to fulfill the capital adequacy ratio requirement within the not too tight time schedule of three years also came out much lower than expected. The undercapitalization of most banks became evident, and the government was confronted with the problem of dealing with the banks as such instead of trying to set new standards for the financial sector in general as early as in late 1991. *Emergency landing could not be ruled out anymore.*

3   Banking reform

The reform of the Hungarian banking sector took place in several steps and it is probable the reform lacked a consistent strategic background. Elements of financial help, efforts towards increasing banking discipline and the slowly increasing acceptance of the necessity of overall bank privatization by the government could be parallelly detected during this far from straight reform process.

The government had to recognize that most Hungarian commercial banks were unable to cope with the new, stricter banking and accounting requirements and, in a more general approach, to survive on their own. Government help was needed, but the evident risk of moral hazard, fiscal arguments and the possible size of the economic plus political cost of a comprehensive rescue package all seemed to push the government towards a more cautious, gradualistic approach.

The first step towards bank consolidation was taken in late 1991. At this point, the government guaranteed half of the bad loans inherited by the commercial banks whose predecessor had been the National Bank of Hungary. This step already included a certain amount of moral hazard. As such, it might have been considered risky without any background of policy effort towards bank restructuring, but it did not really have a great degree of practical relevance. The banks' economic and legal environment started to deteriorate in a widely visible way between late 1991 and early 1992, and their situation called more and more for concerted government action.

The legislative changes listed above made the low quality of the banks' portfolios more manifest than ever (Szelényi and Ursprung, 1998, p. 9). The government guarantee did not help much, because it soon became obvious that not all bad loans were those inherited from the one-tier banking system. In addition to the portfolio problem, the new rules of asset valuation proved to be a dramatic challenge to the banks. They had to realize that the introduction of the new accounting rules pushed the values of their assets quite much below their original level.

They faced imminent crisis in early 1992. This banking crisis consisted of capital, funding and portfolio problems (Szelényi and Ursprung, 1998, p. 9). The government's subsequent bank rescue action was criticized severely at this time, that is in 1992 and 1993, and this criticism was indubitably justified on pure economics grounds. The package had a high cost and it raised the moral hazard problem to a great extent. It also made it evident that bank consolidation cannot be entirely successful without the appropriate changes in economic policy and state-owned banks cannot become fully fledged players on a financial market where most of the non-financial firms are becoming privately owned.

The bank consolidation programme had two main stages: 1. credit consolidation and 2. debtor consolidation (Szelényi and Ursprung, 1998, pp. 9–10.). During the first stage, between December 1992 and April 1993, the non-performing loans of the state-owned banks with capital adequacy ratios below 7.25 per cent[17] were exchanged for special government securities called consolidation bonds (Surányi, 1998, p. 5). Assets classified as bad prior to 1992 were purchased at 50 per cent of their face value, and the corresponding ratio for assets classified as bad in 1992 was 80 per cent.

> Certain claims against special Hungarian business organizations were purchased at face value, but we were unable to establish which ones belonged to this group of companies. The consolidation bonds themselves were negotiable, 20–year-maturity, adjustable rate bonds indexed to the interest rate of treasury bills (this interest rate was determined by the market only and alone) (Surányi, 1998, p. 5.).

The cost of the first stage of the bank consolidation programme – debt consolidation – cannot be easily established. The combined face value of assets acquired by the government amounted to approx. USD 1.4 billion, and the government paid for them with approx. USD 1.1 billion worth of loan consolidation bonds. Interest on these bonds is due once in a year. The direct cost of this stage of the bank consolidation programme has been these annual payments of interest, but its indirect cost was the increase of government debt.

The debt consolidation programme continued after 1992 with the restructuring of financial obligations arising from this programme between various agencies of the government and state-owned financial companies. These actions included the resale of a package of bad loans to the state-owned Hungarian Bank of Investment and Development with the objective of a technical cleanup of state debt. This bank then had the choice of rescheduling debts, swapping them for equity or even cancelling them. This could be done technically by a bank, while the government would have been unable to do so owing to regulatory constraints by the Act on State Budget Management.[18]

Government claims of firms were managed by the seller banks on a commissioned basis until 1994. All such claims still kept by the Ministry of Finance on behalf of the government were then sold to privately owned asset management companies, or given into the management of the Hungarian Bank of Investment and Development as well.

This first stage of the bank consolidation programme was basically aimed not at the banks themselves, but at their debtors. Therefore the strategic objective of this stage included a stabilization of the enterprise sector of the economy. In this approach, the bank consolidation programme continued in two different directions:

- Its *microeconomic* branch included an enterprise-oriented loan consolidation programme carried out in 1993 and 1994. This programme had nothing to do with bank consolidation as such, but it also helped in cleaning up the market with a substantial alleviation of the financial burdens of 15 large, mostly state-owned non-financial companies and with partial debt relief offered to 155 smaller companies (part of these finally did not qualify for the programme).
- Its *banking* branch was the first part of the government's consolidation effort covering the financial institutions themselves. When speaking of turbulences, the crisis of the Hungarian banking sector and the efforts towards solving it deserve our special attention.

The size of the Hungarian banking crisis is well shown by the following two indicators:

1 The *ratio balance sheet total/GDP* fell from its maximum, 85 per cent in 1991 to 77 per cent in 1992, 72 per cent in 1993 and 68 per cent in 1994 (Szelényi and Ursprung, 1998, pp. 22–5.).
2 *Total pre-tax profits* of the sector halved from HUF 63 billion (approx. USD 1 billion) in 1990 to 1991 and disappeared by 1992. The result of increasing capital shortages was that, in 1993, Hungarian banks made a combined loss of close to USD 2 billion (Szelényi and Ursprung, 1998, p. 26).

A synthetic figure speaks of the necessity of government intervention towards solving the crisis of the banking sector. In spite of former efforts of debtor consolidation, the portfolio of the problem claims[19] of the banking sector rose to HUF 352 billion (approx. USD 3.5 billion) by the end of 1993, out of which about 52.8 per cent were bad debts combined (Surányi, 1998, p. 6). These quite sizeable data were calculated based on the old Hungarian accounting standards. According to the new ones, the combined value of bad, doubtful and substandard assets was as high as HUF 418 billion (about 19 per cent more than according to the former method), out of which bad debts comprised 58.1 per cent).

All this means debtor consolidation did not really solve the problem. Instead of tackling the banks' clients, *the government had to find appropriate therapy for the banks themselves*. This quite complex therapy was implemented from December 1993,[20] but it came to an end much later than originally predicted. The reason was several banks turned out to be even worse problem cases when their privatization was finally seriously contemplated.

The process took three steps, and the main tool used was consolidation bonds again. The purpose of the process was the *recapitalization of the banks*. The gradual approach applied by the government led to successive increases of the capital adequacy ratios of the banks involved. The final objective was to reach the 8 per cent level according to BIS standards.

First step: eight banks received injections of capital in December 1993. This enabled them to reach capital adequacy ratios of 0 or above. Furthermore, a bank and a savings protection fund were also recapitalized while they obtained subordinated loans. The bill of this first step was HUF 130 billion (approx. USD 1.3 billion).

Second step: this stage of the bank consolidation programme was carried out in May 1994. It was heavily criticized partly because elections to parliament took place in the same time. The then opposition winning the elections expressed its agreement with the idea of bank consolidation afterwards[21] although the technique implemented was not widely accepted. The bill of this second step was much below the first one, only HUF 18 billion. At this time, additional capital was offered to the banks undertaking restructuring, but their state ownership was transferred from the State Asset Management Corporation (the major privatization agency) to the Ministry of Finance. This transfer underlined direct government participation in the action. This recapitalization raised the direct or indirect state ownership stake in almost all banks involved to at least 80 per cent.

Third step: shortly after Stage 2, subordinated loans were granted to four banks. The bill was HUF 15 billion at this time, and capital adequacy ratios of the banks involved increased to 8 per cent in accordance with BIS standards.

It would be mistaken to perceive the bank consolidation programme as an array of subsidy packages without any action by the banks in return. The banks involved were required to carry out restructuring programmes. These latter had to cover bad loans. Portfolio cleanups by the banks included, for example, the creation of asset management companies and the sale of bad loans in packages to these subsidiaries. This was more than a mere technique of optical portfolio cleanup: these bad-asset-management-subsidiaries[22] became players on the capital market on their own right, and some of them was successful in selling some bad assets at discount prices. If we go back to our aeroplane story for a moment, the establishment of these separate asset-management firms resembled such emergency landings before which passengers are asked to throw out fragile or hazardous pieces of baggage from the plane. This is, of course, impossible in modern, airtight jet planes.

It is interesting to note that rescue actions of banks continued after the bank consolidation programme was officially concluded (that is, by the government whose financial experts had spoken against the consolidation programme). Three such rescue actions are worth mention, and each of them served admittedly the subsequent privatization of the banks involved. The first such rescue action took place at Budapest Bank in 1995: capital reduction at the bank was avoided by a transfer of consolidation bonds worth HUF 12 billion (approx. USD 100 million) to the bank. This transfer was conditional upon the bank's privatization by the end of 1995. This privatization took place on schedule, and consolidation bonds were repurchased by the government from the privatization revenue. As a result, the bank was privatized *de facto* at almost zero price. Although this fact was interpreted by the then political opposition as a 'sellout' of national wealth, we would rather be inclined to say that this very low price simply reflected the extremely bad financial condition of the bank.

The second rescue action concerned two medium-size banks whose mere existence had reflected the mushrooming of undercapitalized sectoral banks at the time of the seemingly high profitability of the then oligopolistic banking business in Hungary. Both these banks, Agrobank and Mezőbank, were serving agriculture and both were on the verge of bankruptcy in early 1996. Their consolidation included their merger, at the time of which they received a capital injection of HUF 9 billion.

Moreover, the government offered guarantees for their bad assets transferred to asset-management companies.

The third rescue action was still under way in early 1999, and therefore it can be only outlined in rather vague terms. The bank involved is the second largest player of the Hungarian banking business, Postabank. This bank was the first element of privately owned banking in Hungary: it was established in 1988 with a minority ownership stake of the Austrian Postsparkasse (Post Savings Bank).[23] It became thereafter the strongest rival on the Hungarian market of the former monopolist in retail banking, OTP (Szelényi and Ursprung, 1998, p. 16).

The bank's management built up considerable political influence and a wide range of business clients, but this very ambitious and widespread networking effort gradually led to a deterioration of the quality of the bank's portfolio. The bank suffered a serious liquidity crisis in 1997, and the government taking power in 1998 immediately replaced its board and management. The new structures of corporate governance disclosed pieces of distorted information in balance sheets, and the Assembly General of December 1998 decided a re-nationalization of the bank following a significant reduction of capital. The expected need for capital injection from the government is in the range of USD 1.1–1.2 billion. The total cost of the rescue package is estimated to increase the relative share of budget deficit in GDP by more than 1 percentage point.

This very telling example speaks of an important new and quite surprising reason of financial turbulences in a transition economy. It shows that *problems related to the mismanagement of banks are not a privilege limited to state ownership, but its adverse financial consequences may fall back on the government.* If the government would refrain from rescue action in Postabank's case, it would seriously threaten the stability of the entire Hungarian banking system. The Postabank case proves that the private ownership of banks is not a safe guarantee of the stability of the banking system if banking supervision is not strict enough.

It is still a topic for analysis (and/or discussion) whether banking supervision did not alert the government because it was underinformed or because it feared political intervention on behalf of the bank's former board and management. Another crucial problem for a more mature stage of the transition process arises from this question: it seems that the mere establishment of legal checks and balances in the economy and also in the financial sector does not necessarily create the expected level of transparency of competition and security of investment (or ownership).

Competition policy and banking or capital markets supervision in transition countries should be put to closer scrutiny in this respect by further research.

This research should have a legal and insitutional character in order to see the extent to which guarantees of the real political independence of the supervising agencies are effective or not.

Strong formal guarantees exist for the political independence of the agencies in point but the real content of these guarantees may not be entirely clear.

The privatization of the other large Hungarian banks has to be assessed in light of the Postabank case. The five other large banks were largely privatized between 1994 and 1998:

- MKB (Hungarian Foreign Trade Bank Ltd) became a subsidiary of Bayerische Landesbank of Germany;
- OTP Bank (National Savings and Commercial Bank), by far the leading Hungarian retail bank was privatized in several stages. Part of its shares was introduced to the stock exchange, other portions of equity were sold to foreign institutional investors, small Hungarian private investors, and transferred to domestic social security funds or municipalities. This is the only large Hungarian commercial bank out of the five without any strong majority owner;
- Budapest Bank's majority owner is a consortium of General Electric Capital of the United States and the EBRD;
- Hungarian Credit Bank was 90 per cent privatized with an acquisition by ABN-AMRO Bank of the Netherlands. Its former Hungarian managers now play a key role in Hungarian economic policymaking. For example, its last Hungarian President-CEO, Zsigmond Járai, has been Hungary's finance minister since July 1998;
- K&H Bank (Commercial and Credit Bank) was the last large Hungarian bank to be privatized. This acquisition took place in late 1997, and the bank's new foreign owners are the Irish Life insurance company and Kredietbank of Belgium.

Our short but comprehensive list of the prestigious new owners of the large Hungarian banks might make it likely that none of them would allow their Hungarian subsidiary to the verge of Postabank-like disaster. Still, the strengthening of supervisory agencies in banking and other fields of the financial sector remains a key task of the government.

4   Conclusions

Twelve years have passed since Hungary established or rather re-established its two-tier banking system. This spectacular and widely welcomed action was the beginning of a comprehensive reform of the financial sector. A series of turbulences followed, many of which could be considered a by-product of the transition process:

- the slump of the early nineties combined with soaring inflation was, for example, a result of drastic import liberalization and the loss of traditional export markets;
- the dramatic deterioration of the quality of the portfolio of the commercial banks followed from a former strategic mistake committed by the government: the two-tier banking system was created on a state-owned basis and the lack of transparent criteria for lending combined with *de facto* missing corporate governance made the outflow of credits to low-quality debtors a regular practice;
- legal changes belonging to the transition process made life more difficult for commercial banks in 1992, and their true condition and performance became visible. As a result, most of them turned out to be unable to survive without government help. The bank consolidation process had to be completed with the privatization of all commercial banks in Hungary.

We have seen that the private ownership of a commercial bank is no true remedy to poor performance and is no absolute preventive against consolidation from the state budget. Still, the Postabank case speaks mainly of an as yet neglected task of the transition process: the fact that the government gave up ownership in nearly all commercial banks should mean that it should strengthen its regulatory and supervisory function considerably. Knowing that, besides the quality of the portfolios of the banks *the quality of their owners* also matters.

The integration of most Hungarian banks into multinational networks of banking systems offers a strong guarantee in this respect. The relative share of qualified assets within the portfolio of the Hungarian banking sector decreased considerably between 1994 and the first half of 1998, as shown in Figure 12.4.

This very favourable structural change can be mainly traced back to the massive privatization programme of the Hungarian banking sector. It does not, however, mark the end of financial turbulences in the economy. The crash of the Budapest Stock Exchange in August-September 1998 manifested itself in a 60 per cent fall of BUX (the Budapest Stock Exchange index). This crash meant that the Hungarian financial sector was now open and liberalized enough to react immediately to turbulences abroad. This ability to react was a very important

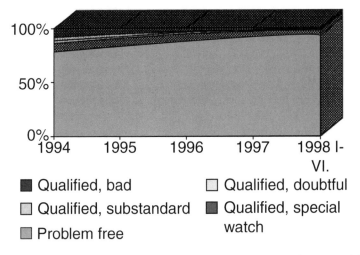

Figure 12.4   The structure of the Hungarian banking sector's combined portfolio (1994–98, %)
Source: National Bank of Hungary (adapted from Surányi, 1998, p. 18).

result of the transition process or, to borrow a term from philosophy, kind of a synthesis of former turbulences and reform steps in response to them.

All in all, the aeroplane of the Hungarian financial sector did not crash. It had to carry out an emergency landing in response to major safety problems during turbulence, but this costly and lengthy emergency landing[24] helped prevent disaster. Now, again in the air with a stronger mechanical structure and with more fuel-efficient engines, it would react to turbulences with much less discomfort in the passenger cabin. As a matter of fact, BUX gained back two thirds of its fall in last summer's crash between September 1998 and January 1999.

Notes

1   Cf. *Business Central Europe*, December 1998/January 1999, 46–7.
2   Data on foreign debt for the 1980s mostly reflected gross debt due to the fact that dollar-denominated Hungarian credits included such government aid disguised in credits to Communist-oriented Third World countries whose repayment had been and remained out of the question.
3   The last year of more than 2 per cent growth before 1987 had been 1978. It is due to the existence of such a long period of poor Hungarian growth performance that we are very sceptical about any kind of time comparisons speaking

of reaching 1989, 1975 or whatsoever levels of GDP volume in the years to come.

4   This borrowing was not used to buy Soviet oil directly. It was mainly used for financing investment generating exports of manufactured goods to the Soviet market but not sellable elsewhere.

5   The year of the second Hungarian pricing reform. For details of the reform process see (Brada, Singh and Török, 1994, pp. 3–7).

6   For an in-depth comparison of the macroeconomic performances of the CEECs cf. (Begg, 1998).

7   Not to be found in economic policy literature but experienced by this author several times.

8   Antall died in office, in December 1993.

9   A good example for this government attitude was an element of its fiscal policy: the simple purchase of government bonds was considered as part of tax-deductible savings in 1993 and 1994 if the bonds were held for three years at least. This measure was withdrawn in late 1994 *before* the shock therapy package.

10 For the Polish case partially analogous with the Hungarian one see (Chudzik, 1998). For Hungary, probably the best overview of the problem in English is offered by (Szelényi and Ursprung, 1998).

11 At an informal meeting in 1992, a top Hungarian banker summarized this problem in an aphoristic way: 'The firms asking for credits from me are ones I don't want to give credits to; the firms I want to give credits to are ones not asking for credits from me'.

12 We know of a major electronics firm with 20 000 employees which invested USD 10 million into a Soviet market oriented project around 1988. The project completely failed because it was technically impossible to find alternative markets after 1990. Not even spare parts piled up for the project could be resold, and the whole amount of banking loans aimed at the project turned into the worst form of bad debt in 1990–91. The company went into liquidation in late 1991.

13 A good explanation of the seemingly high, but in fact illusory profits of Hungarian banks is offered by (Szelényi and Ursprung, 1998, p. 9). They explain, for example, that pre-1991 regulation allowed outstanding interest revenue (quite high in the given inflationary environment) to be recorded as profit on which tax and dividends were paid.

14 One reason for this reluctance to proceed to shock therapy including devaluation and a string of measures of drastic liberalization may have been the negative impressions the Hungarian public opinion had of the consequences of the Polish shock therapy implemented in 1990 by Leszek Balcerowicz. In the same time, the seemingly good Czech experience with cautious reform measures could be interpreted as corroborating the Hungarian government's choice of experimenting with legal measures first.

15 The analysis of the legal pieces is drawn from (Surányi, 1998, p. 3). Comments and assessments are ours.

16 The benefit of this measure became evident at the time of the stock exchange crisis in September 1998 when the only securities' traders unable to survive the bear period were those not backed by strong commercial banks. In other words: all brokerage houses linked to banks survived.

17 These banks included 14 commercial banks and 69 savings cooperatives, i.e. many more financial institutions than the ones created with the establishment of the two-tier banking system.

18 Literally translated from Hungarian, it could be called 'State Household Act'.

19 Bad, doubtful and substandard assets.

20 The description of the programme is based on (Surányi, 1998, p. 7).

21 To be more precise: its inevitability was acknowledged. Professional (i.e. non-political) criticism was focused on the fact that this consolidation programme injected money into the economy formally circumventing the state budget (cf. Hetényi, 1995, p. 22).

22 The name of at least one of them was very telling: Risk Ltd.

23 Even in 1999, it is not clearly defined by transition literature whether the acquisition of a formerly state-owned firm by a foreign, fully or partly state-owned company could be considered privatization or not.

24 The bank consolidation process.

References and further reading

Antalóczy, K. (1996) A hosszú csatlakozás. Magyarország útja a Bretton Woods-i intézményekhez, *Külgazdaság*, 40, 9, 65–75.

Antalóczy, K., Gáspár, P., Mohácsi, K. and Várhegyi, É. (1998) A tőkebeáramlások kezelése, Manuscript, *Pénzügykutató Rt.*, Budapest, February, 131.

Barabás, G., Hamecz, I. and Neményi, J. (1998) A költségvetés finanszírozási rendszerének átalakítása és az eladósodás megfékezése II, *Közgazdasági Szemle*, 45, 789–802.

Begg, D. (1998) Dezinfláció Közép-és Kelet-Európában: az eddigi tapasztalatok, in C. Cottarelli and G. Szapáry (eds), 114–35.

Bonin, J. P. (1996) Átalakulóban a bankszféra: a magyar, a lengyel és a cseh bank-privatizáció, *Külgazdaság*, 40, 7–8, 11–38.

Brada, J. C., Singh, I. and Török, Á. (1994) *Firms Afloat and Firms Adrift. Hungarian Industry and the Economic Transition*, Armonk-London: M.E. Sharpe, 104.

Chudzik, R. (1998) Banking Regulation versus Market Discipline? In Search for an Appropriate Framework for Banking Systems in Eastern Europe, in E. Miklaszewska (ed.), *Global Tendencies and Changes in East European Banking*, Cracow: Jagiellonian University, 225–44.

Cottarelli, C. and Szapáry, G. (eds) (1998) *Mérsékelt infláció. Az átalakuló gazdaságok tapasztalatai*, National Bank of Hungary, 255.

Gál, P. (1998) A bankrendszer átrendeződése és az euro, *Közgazdasági Szemle*, 45, December, 1112–25.

Hetényi, I. (1996) *Államháztartási reform. Tények és gondok 1995 végén*, Budapest: Ministry of Finance, January, 43.

Jarociński, M. (1998) Money Demand and Monetization in Transition Economies, *CASE-CEU Working Papers Series*, no. 13, Warsaw, September, 38.

Jelentés az infláció…(1998) *Jelentés az infláció alakulásáról*, National Bank of Hungary, November, 97.

Kosterna, U. (1998) On the Road to the European Union. Some Remarks on the Budget. The Performance in Transition Economies, *CASE-CEU Working Papers Series*, no. 1, Warsaw, 1998, 40.

Krzak, M. (1998) Large Current Account Deficits – The Case of Central Europe and the Baltic States, Oesterreichische Nationalbank, *Focus on Transition*, 1, Vienna: OeNB, 22–46.

Miklaszewska, E. (ed.) (1998) *Global Tendencies and Changes in East European Banking*, Cracow: Jagiellonian University, 405.

NBH (1997) *National Bank of Hungary Annual Report 1996*, Budapest, June 1997, 268.

NBH (1998) *National Bank of Hungary Annual Report 1997*, Budapest, June 1998, 325.

North, D. C. (1997) The Contribution of the New Institutional Economics to the Understanding of the Transition Problem. UN University WIDER, *Annual Lectures*, 1, Helsinki, March, 18.

Orlowski, L. T. (1998) Monetary Policy Targeting in Central Europe's Transition Economies: The Case for Direct Inflation Targeting, *CASE-CEU Working Papers Series*, no. 11, Warsaw, August, 30.

Petschnig, M. Z. (ed.) (1998), Hegymenet. Jelentés a magyar gazdaság 1997. évi folyamatairól, *Pénzügykutató Rt.*, Budapest, 173.

Sgard, J. (1996) Foreign Debt Settlements in Bulgaria, Hungary and Poland, 1989–1996, in C. Helmenstein (ed.), *Capital Markets in Transition Economies*, Aldershot: Edward Elgar.

Stiglitz, J. E. (1998) More Instruments and Broader Goals: Moving toward the Post-Washington Consensus, UN University WIDER, *Annual Lectures*, 2. Helsinki, 1998, 40.

Surányi, G. (1998) Restructuring the Banking Sector in Hungary. The Vienna Institute of International Economic Studies (WIIW). Paper prepared for the WIIW 25 Years Anniversary Conference, Vienna, 11–13 November, Manuscript, 18.

Surányi, G. and Vincze, J. (1998) Infláció Magyarországon (1990–1997), in C. Cottarelli and G. Szapáry (eds), 140–58.

Szelényi, E. and Ursprung, J. (1998) *The Hungarian Two-Tier Banking System. The First Eleven Years (1987–1997)*, National Bank of Hungary, August, 35.

The Hungarian Banking . . . (1998) *The Hungarian Banking Sector. Developments in 1997*, Budapest: National Bank of Hungary, 20.

Urban, L. (1998) Trade-offs between Macro-performance and Micro-restructuring in Transition Economies: Contrasting the Czech and the Hungarian Experience, *CASE-CEU Working Papers Series*, 5, Warsaw, June, 35.

Viszt, E. (1997) A magyar gazdaság teljesítménye a Maastrichti Szerzodés konvergenciakritériumainak tükrében, *Külgazdaság*, 41, 7–8, 4–21.

Woĉniak, P. (1998) Relative Price Adjustment in Poland, Hungary and the Czech Republic. Comparison of the Size and Impact on Inflation, *CASE-CEU Working Papers Series*, 12, Warsaw, August, 47.

Zsámboki, B. (1998) *A bankrendszer jövõje (egy kérdõíves felmérés alapján)*, MNB, Budapest, February, 27.

13
Comment on Török

Johannes Stephan

Török's chapter is a comprehensive analysis of the Hungarian financial sector crisis and developments since 1986. To its advantage, it contains an additional criterion which usually remains neglected in the vast amount of literature on this matter. He refers to it as 'an element of Hungarian government philosophy': Hungary's bias of legal regulation over macroeconomic reform or transition policy. Török rightly stresses that in any analysis concerned with the reform of the Hungarian financial sector, this aspect should command central consideration.

Török is in good company when critically assessing the costs and benefits of Hungarian financial sector reforms and crisis management, as well as the deficit in banking supervision. His chapter could be read to hold the hypothesis that better supervision could have prevented some of the detrimental effects of the various crisis. In the end, however, Török holds that emergency landings were largely successful as they did not demand a toll too high for the functioning of Hungary's financial sector. The plane underwent comprehensive repairs and was subsequently able to take off on a more secure flight this time.

In agreement with Török on most aspects of his fine chapter, my task in commenting on it can only be to accentuate two of the main points raised in his analysis.

1   The two-tier banking system and interbank competition

Hungary's systemic transformation and the reformation of its financial sector is a particular one clearly distinguishable from reforms in other post-socialist economies. The dissolution of the socialist financial system that comprised solely of one omnipotent monobank was commenced in 1987, well before more comprehensive reforms were carried through in such vigour. But while this reform is generally held to have aimed at the promotion of interbank competition which in turn was to ensure efficiency in the operation of the financial sector, this most fundamental reform served foremost the fulfilment of *the* paramount condition for the functioning of a monetary constitution in a modern monetary economy. Only divorce of the money supply from commercial crediting can systemically attach a value on scarce 'money' and a price on 'credit' (contrived scarcity and hard budget constraint). Indeed, the central bank was henceforth required to align the supply of money to its task of guarding the value of the national currency, the Forint, clearly stated in its mandate.

Interbank competition nevertheless remains relevant, not least with respect to monetary stabilization and the credibility of the financial system: the efficient allocation of capital to profit-making economic activities that are able to pay back loans by employing eco-nomic resources *and* earn profit, crucially depends on a competitive market that selects investors according to the quality of their investment plans. The ability to select viable debtors determines the extent of stability of the inherently unstable new financial system. This mechan-ism is of particular relevance in post-socialist economies, as here the stock of old loans does not, by all means, reflect debtor-creditworthiness. The fact that after the dissolution of the monobank, commercial banks were unable to roll-over existing credits to insuffi-ciently creditworthy client-companies (which applied to the vast major-ity of debtors then) further increased the instability of the Hungarian financial system.

Interbank competition, however, did not emerge as had largely been expected. The following statistics on the Hungarian financial system highlight that the splitting of the Hungarian monobank might be considered a necessary condition for emerging interbank competition, but proved to be rather insufficient. The Hungarian policy of a quasi-surgical separation of the three central bank credit divisions from the National Bank of Hungary into independent commercial banks in effect guaranteed them a monopoly position. The 'new' commercial banks appeared to be nothing else than the former branches of the state monobank.

The 'new' commercial banks (or former regional branches of the state monobank) enjoyed a dominant market position: back in 1988, they shared 54 per cent of total assets in the system, adding the national savings bank OTP, the figure even rises to 91 per cent, a highly segre-gated market with little room for competition.

It is therefore little surprise that profits were, as Török puts it, 'astronomical': proudly quoted by the central bank, a survey published in *The Banker* in 1991 puts five Hungarian banks within the group of the 1000 strongest banks in the world. While these 1000 banks could generate an average ratio of net income before taxes to total assets of 0.54 in 1990, the average ratio of Hungarian banks achieved an astonishing value of 3.90.

The banks' structure of clientele allowed them to operate virtually without competition from other banks during the first few years of their 'new' existence. In 1989, private households allocated their savings overwhelmingly with the OTP, the shares of the groups of large banks and medium-sized banks were negligible. Enterprises, also concentrated on large banks, but here medium-sized banks could already attract a significant share. This structure holds equally true for the loans taken out from financial institutions by households and enterprises.

Only 2 years later, the structure was much more balanced. To understand the figures properly, however, it is important to note that emerging economic activity in small private enterprises was not yet reflected in the figures for the enterprise sector, but remained within the classification of the household sector.

Banks' portfolios were largely undiversified, with each bank concentrating on one particular industry or branch; the system therefore became increasingly vulnerable to asymmetric shocks. In the extreme case, a bank had only a few major clients with something like a

Table 13.1 Profitability indices of Hungarian financial institutions

(end of 1990)	Profit (Ft bn)	Profit ratio to total assets (%)	Profit ratio to equity (%)	Profit per employee (Ft million)	Total assets per employee (Ft million)
Large banks	30.7	3.94	56.27	3.25	82.61
Medium-size banks	11.7	4.91	41.62	4.82	98.14
Specialist FI	2.3	5.35	14.09	7.27	135.96
Hungarian-owned FI	55.9	3.84	60.23	2.22	57.99
Joint Venture-FI	7.4	4.50	32.14	6.61	146.87
OTP	18.5	3.32	111.03	1.32	39.78
Total	63.3	3.90	54.66	2.41	61.8

Source: National Bank of Hungary.

Table 13.2 Segmentation of loans and deposits by economic actors (%)

| | Loans | | | | Deposits | | | |
| | Household loans | | Enterprises loans | | Household deposits | | Enterprise deposits | |
(end of...)	1989	1991	1989	1991	1989	1991	1989	1991
Large banks	1	78	80	68	1	76	70	65
Medium banks	1	1	14	21	2	7	9	22
Small banks	0	0	2	9	0	3	2	12
OTP	98	21	4	2	97	14	19	1

Source: Stephan, 1999, 125.

key-account status or even rather more: regardless of existing bankruptcy laws, an enterprise that found itself in financial difficulties could depend on its bank for bail-out, as the survival of the enterprise was closely linked to the survival of the bank. The central bank's function *vis-à-vis* the banks to act as lender of last resort closes the vicious circle.

In addition to insufficient interbank competition, Hungary's financial institutions developed a particular *modus operandi* which served to further destabilize the system as a whole. Faced with insufficient profit from its lending business (or even losses, as some of the loans to bankrupt or liquidated companies had to be written off), banks retained their ability to meet their financial obligations, for example for interest payments to their depositors, by attracting further deposits. It is immediately clear that this would become increasingly problematic in as much as the volume of deposits would have to rise constantly to assure the functioning of that policy.

2 The bad-asset problem and the Hungarian consolidation schemes

The second most prominent speciality about the Hungarian financial sector reforms is how the issue of un-performing, or even uncollectible assets in banks' portfolios were dealt with. Considering the detrimental combination of insufficient interbank competition and of transformational recession on enterprises' competitiveness and creditworthiness, it is not surprising that the amount of credits outstanding from debtors rose. The above outlined structure proves that banks' survival was too closely linked with the survival of their clients. True, the newly installed banks inherited some 'uncollectible assets' in their portfolios. The escalation of the problem of 'bad assets', however, emerged only in the subsequent period and appears to be a common feature in all post-socialist economies and can be traced back to the selective socialist way to grant credits to enterprises via the state-owned monobank-system: rather than selecting profitable enterprises, usually enterprises that could not fulfil their share of the plans or were otherwise of national interest were supplied with capital, credits these companies never had to worry about paying back in the framework of the old system.

The skyrocketing of bad assets has to be attributed not so much to a general lack in managerial know-how (insufficient evaluation of debtors' creditworthiness, debt-equity swaps, etc.), but rather to the above stylised malfunctioning of the financial market governed by the banking system. The quality of banks' assets typically suffers during phases of economic recession, but to make matters worse, Hungary's recession was paired with a high interest rate-policy on behalf of the central bank in its attempt to reduce inflation (see Figure 13.1).

The above provided stylized facts clearly raise the question of banking supervision to assure prudential operation of commercial banks. Török holds in his chapter that 'the strengthening of supervisory agencies in banking and other fields of the financial sector remains a key task for the government'.

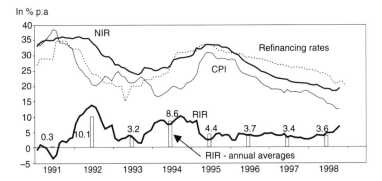

Figure 13.1 Hungary's nominal and real interest rates and inflation
Notes: Nominal (NIR) and real (RIR) are for maturities for less than one year. Real interest rates are *ex-post* rates and have been calculated by use of the inflation rate (CPI). Refinancing rates until and including 1992 are rates against the provision of foreign currency collateral and since 1993 are repo-rates maturing in less than one week.
Source: National Bank of Hungary.

It remains uncertain, however, whether improved regulation of commercial banking activity could have actually prevented the persistent expansion of uncollectible bank assets without unduly aggravating Hungary's transformational recession. Nevertheless, banking supervision commands particular importance in the case of the transition economies, as here, credibility and trust in its stability within a framework of an unstable macroeconomic situation tends to be weak. Banking supervision in transition economies, therefore, has to *exceed rather than catch-up* to the usual scope of control in mature financial markets made indispensable by the fact that modern financial systems are inherently unstable anyway.

Finally, Török stresses that 'Solutions provided to these crises proved more or less durable and defensible in debates with the economics profession'. The following calculations by the Hungarian State Banking Supervision Authority underpin that assessment with respect to the consolidation programmes designed to solve the problem of 'bad assets'. The analysis compares the development of average capital adequacy ratios of the Hungarian banking system in two scenarios with and without consolidation efforts. The speculative assessment of the scenario without consolidation efforts simply assumes that all classified assets remained with the banks, and no capital had been injected into the banks or debtor enterprises, other things, as usual, remaining equal. Table 13.3 quite clearly proves that the ratios would have eroded without, but rather improved markedly with execution of the three Hungarian consolidation efforts.

A similar attempt can be made by looking at the development of the amount of bad assets in the same two scenarios, one with and the other without consolidation efforts. The method of speculation remains the same as above. Table 13.4 again clearly underpins the positive assessment of Hungary's consolidation programmes in their aim to reduce the burden of the low quality of banks' assets.

Table 13.3 The development of capital adequacy ratios of the Hungarian banking sector between 1992 and 1994

	1992		1993		1994	
	Without consolidation	With consolidation	Without consolidation	With consolidation	Without consolidation	With consolidation
Ratio	0.01	8.83	16.80	11.18	17.28	15.51

Source: State Banking Supervisory Authority.

Table 13.4 Development of bank assets according to risk

	Total assets	Bad debts	Bad, doubtful and sub-standard	Bad debts	Bad, doubtful and sub-standard
		Under consideration of the schemes		As if no consolidation took place	
31 Dec. 1992[1]					
	1637.4	184.5 (11.3)	286.4 (17.5)	184.5 (11.3)	286.4 (17.5)
31 Dec. 1994[2]					
	2440.4	218.5 (9.0)	344.0 (14.1)	545.0 (22.3)	670.5 (27.5)
Index	149.0	118.4	120.0	295.4	234.1

Notes: The figures in brackets represent the proportion of classified assets in total assets.
[1] Figures are nominated in Ft billion and reflect the stocks *before* the introduction of any consolidation scheme.
[2] Figures are denominated in Ft billion and reflect the stocks *after* the completion of the various consolidation schemes.
Sources: National Bank of Hungary, own calculations.

Conclusions

Today, Hungary's financial sector in general and the banking system in particular are held to be the most stable ones among post-socialist economies. Average capital adequacy ratios are healthy and reach nearly double the amount legally required, and bank profits are on the rise again despite narrowing interest rate margins. All this is certainly attributable to some extent to national policies that aimed at consolidating banks' balance sheets. What should not be overlooked in that respect, however, is that Hungary's financial sector is largely privatized which is attributable not least to the fact that the Hungarian government substantially opened the domestic financial market to foreign competition, allowing foreign banks to engage financially in Hungarian banks or even set up own subsidiaries. Today, the majority of shares in banks operating in Hungary are held by foreigners while the share of the state fell below 20 per cent. Remarkably, the strategy to privatize banks by way of liberalization and subsequently their submission to international competition did not result in the demise of domestic banks.

With respect to financial turbulences in Hungary, however, one final remark should receive attention: back in 1994–95 during Hungary's economic recovery with healthy growth rates, the economy nearly fell prey to financial crises comparable to the ones in the Czech Republic in May 1997 and Russia in late 1998. Hungary's current account deteriorated to unsustainable levels, and the state budget, not least due to the financial burdens from the consolidations efforts and the renewed increase in nominal interest rates, let expenditure exceed revenues to unprecedented levels. When inflation and devaluation pressures began to pick up in late 1994, the then new government enacted a comprehensive rescue programme which showed positive results on all fronts almost immediately. In 1995, Hungary proved to be able to weather the storm of a financial crisis on the horizon.

Revisiting today the focus of the 1995–programme on the 'twin deficit', however, the danger of a renewed financial destabilization seems to be not much less imminent than in 1995. First estimates for 1998 show that the trade balance and with it the current account deficit appear to be escalating yet again, possibly surpassing the psychological level of 5 per cent of GDP (see Table 13.5). Parallel to that development, the state budget will have again grown out of control. This time, the blame is not so much on exceeding interest payments, as first estimates of the primary budget surplus, i.e. the one excluding interest and principal payments on debt, is less than half the value of the previous year.

Is Hungary heading into an unsustainable financial situation a second time? Will the government, in the wake of EU membership, yet again have to consider tough anti-crisis measures, that curbed growth back in 1995 and 1996? Or will the undoubtedly improved credibility of Hungary's financial sector be able to draw sufficient foreign capital to balance the current account and the state budget? In that case, that is, the continuation of the capital import-based transformation strategy, however, Hungary might well continue to linger on the verge of crisis due to the burden of rising foreign debts and profit repatriation from

Table 13.5 Real growth and the 'twin deficit' (% of GDP)

	1990	1991	1992	1993	1994	1995	1996	1997	1998
State budget	0.4	2.2	7.1	6.0	8.4	6.7	3.1	4.1	6.8
Primary budget	n/a	n/a	n/a	n/a	2.7	1.6	4.3	3.1	1.4
Trade balance	1.1	0.6	0.1	8.4	8.8	5.5	5.9	3.9	7 3
Current account	0.4	0.8	0.9	9.0	9.4	5.6	3.7	2.2	5 7
Real Growth (in %, p.a.)	3.5	11.9	3.0	0.8	2.9	1.5	1.3	4.6	5.1

Note: Figures for 1998 are estimates.

Sources: National Bank of Hungary, EBRD, own calculations.

past foreign direct investment on the state budget and the balance of payments. With the Hungarian financial markets having reached a reassuring level of maturity, the time might be ripe for the international capital markets to get more say in the decision over the appropriate exchange rate of the Forint. Not least, this could put an end to Hungary's currency overvaluation and might improve the economy's external position.

References

European Bank of Reconstruction and Development, various issues of Transition Reports, London.

National Bank of Hungary, various issues of Annual and Monthly Reports, as well as non-periodical publications, Budapest.

State Banking Supervisory Authority, various issues of Annual Reports, Budapest.

Stephan, J. (1999) *Economic Transition in Hungary and East Germany – Gradualism, Shock Therapy and Catch-Up Development*, Basingstoke: Macmillan and New York: St Martin's Press.

14
Comment on Török

Uwe Vollmer

1. Professor Török uses in his chapter a nice allegory: He compares the Hungarian economy with an airline company and the Hungarian banking sector with an airplane leased by the airline. In the 1990s this 'aircraft' came into heavy turbulences and Professor Török asks for the reasons for these financial difficulties of Hungarian banks. He argues that 'in-flight dangers' of Hungarian banks did not come from 'bad weather conditions', that is from causes that were exogenous to the Hungarian economy. Financial turbulences were rather the combined result of an array of organizational problems inside the Hungarian economy and a wrong incentive structure for the banking system.

In the mid-1990s the Hungarian legislature learned from these mistakes and ordered an 'emergency landing' for the Hungarian banking system. Among other reforms the Government started a massive privatization programme of the banking sector which resulted in a successful transition process. In November 1998 the EU commission praised Hungary as the best performer in economic transition, including the financial part of the process.

2. I liked reading the chapter very much (especially I liked the use of the airline allegory) and I share the major conclusions, so I do not comment on them. What I want to comment on, because I feel it is left open in the chapter, is an answer to the following question: 'Why is banking reform so important for economic transition?'. The paper gives a hint on the answer to this question because it argues that state-owned banks are subject to moral hazard and therefore unable to fulfill their economic functions properly.

One of these functions, which is stressed in the literature on financial intermediation (Diamond, 1984; Leland and Pyle, 1977), is that banks offer efficient monitoring services to enterprises. They allow would-be-entrepreneurs to raise external capital much cheaper than by direct finance and help firms with little equity capital to get external finance. Because the emergence of new enterprises is very important for a country like Hungary the banking sector plays a very crucial role in economic transition.

This point can be formalized within the principal-agent approach of Holmstrom and Tirole (1997). Although this model does not deal with the economic transition process explicitly it can be used to clarify the problems at issue. The model has three types of agents: firms, intermediaries and outside investors. There are two periods: In the first period all decisions are made and contracts are signed, and in the second period investment returns are realized. All actors are risk neutral, and there is limited liability so no one can end up with a negative cash flow.

There is a continuum of firms which start out with different amounts of equity capital A. Each firm has access to the same project and it costs $I > 0$ in period 1 to undertake the project, so that each firm needs at least $(I - A)$ of external funds to invest. The project can be either a success or a failure. If it is a success it generates a financial return $R > 1$ in period 2; if it is a failure it generates nothing. Table 14.1 shows the flow of funds in periods 1 and 2.

Table 14.1   Flow of funds in the Holmstrom–Tirole model

	T=0	T=1
Success	$-I$	$R > 0$
Failure	$-I$	0

Firms are run by entrepreneurs who can influence the probability of success of the project by hidden action (shirking) and create a moral hazard problem. If the entrepreneur is diligent the probability of success for the project is p_H and he gets no private benefits. If he is lazy the probability of success is $P_L < P_H$ (with $\Delta p = p_H - p_L$) and he receives a private benefit $b > 0$ from being lazy. If he is very lazy the probability of success is still p_L but the entrepreneur receives a private benefit $B > b$. By assumption either level of laziness produces the same probability of success. Therefore the entrepreneur always prefers the high private benefit situation (being very lazy) over the low private benefit situation (being lazy) if he is not monitored. Table 14.2 shows the success probabilities and private benefits depending on the actions chosen by the

Table 14.2 Success probabilities and private benefits

Entrepreneur is	...diligent	...lazy	...very lazy
Private benefit	0	b	B
Probability of success	p_H	p_L	p_L

entrepreneur. By assumption the project is economically viable only if the entrepreneur behaves diligently.

Financial intermediaries (banks) can monitor entrepreneurs and thereby alleviate the moral hazard problem. If they prevent entrepreneurs from being very lazy they reduce the firms' opportunity costs of being diligent from B to b. Monitoring is costly however and the intermediary has to pay an amount c > 0 in order to eleminate the B-outcome of the project. Because this monitoring activity is non-verifiable for outsiders there is a potential moral hazard problem for banks too. This moral hazard forces intermediaries to inject some of their own capital into the firm that they monitor making the aggregate amount of intermediary (or 'informed') capital K_m an important constraint on aggregate investments. Outside investors are uninformed and do not control firms and banks. They demand an expected rate of return γ.

Holmstrom and Tirole (1997, 670–6) argue that there are two critical values, $\underline{A}$ and $\bar{A}$, for the firm's equity capital as shown in Figure 14.1 which measures A on the horizontal axis:

- Only firms with $A \geq \bar{A}$ ('high-capitalized firms') can invest using direct finance, because they can pay outside investors an expected rate of return γ and entrepreneurs receive a share of the project revenue R which is high enough to generate an incentive to behave diligently.

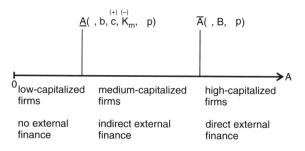

Figure 14.1 Firm's equity capital and external finance

- Firms with $\underline{A} \le A < \bar{A}$ ('medium-capitalized firms') can invest using indirect finance, because outside investors receive an expected rate of return γ, banks receive an expected return that is high enough to encourage them to monitor the firm, and entrepreneurs receive a share of R which is high enough to to generate an incentive to behave diligently.
- Firms with $A < \underline{A}$ ('low-capitalized firms') do not get external finance at all.

3.   In terms of this model transition economies, like Hungary, have the problem that $\underline{A}$ is lying very near to $\bar{A}$. The range of medium-capitalized firms which have access to intermediated finance is too small. Perhaps this was what the top Hungarian banker, cited in note 11 of Professor Török's chapter, meant who said: 'The firms asking for credits from me are ones I don't want to give credits to (because their capital is too small to behave diligently, U.V.); the firms I want give credits to are ones not asking credit from me (because they have access to direct finance; U.V.).'

What are the reasons for a high value $\underline{A}$ in transition economies? Figure 14.1 shows on which parameters in the Holmstrom–Tirole model the critical values $\underline{A}$ (and $\bar{A}$) depend. Two of them are mentioned in the chapter:

- High and increasing monitoring costs c of banks due to static and dynamic internal (X-) inefficiencies of Hungarian banks because of overstaffing and dispersed branch networks.
- Undercapitalization of most Hungarian banks, that is a small value K_m of informed capital that the bank can invest into the firm that it monitors.

If c is high or K_m is low banks need a great share of the project revenue R to control the company properly; then, the entrepreneur behaves only diligently, if he has a great stake A in his own company.

What kinds of financial reforms are necessary to improve on the situation? I do not think that prudential regulations, like minimum reserve ratios, are helpful because they increase the bank's monitoring costs c and therefore increase the critical value $\underline{A}$. Maybe this is a reason for the failure of the 'legislative shock therapy' in Hungary in the early 1990s. Governmental rescue actions are no proper measures too because they increase moral hazard inside banks and soften their budget constraints. On the contrary I think that less state intervention but privatization and more competition between banks are of special importance.

Competition reduces internal inefficiencies of banks and privatization increases the amount of informed capital K_m through acquisition of domestic banks by foreign banks.

4.   In concluding, let me repeat that I enjoyed reading this well-written chapter very much. It gives a good impression of the importance of financial sector reforms for a successful economic transition. My concern was to underpin this impression with the help of a may-be-applicable formal model.

References

Diamond, D. W. (1984) Financial Intermediation and Delegated Monitoring, *Review of Economic Studies*, 51, 393–414.

Leland, H. and Pyle, D. (1977) Information Asymmetries, Financial Structure, and Financial Intermediation, *Journal of Finance*, 32, 371–87.

Holmstrom, B. and Tirole, J. (1997) Financial Intermediation, Loanable Funds, and the Real Sector, *Quarterly Journal of Economics*, 112, 663–91.

VI
Resumee

15*

Financial Markets in Transition Countries: Problems and Aspirations

Stephen F. Frowen

Mr Chairman, Ladies and Gentlemen

It is a great honour and privilege to give the pre-dinner speech at the conclusion of this unique and I am sure you will all agree most successful conference.

My special thanks are due to Professor Jens Hölscher who kindly invited me to address you tonight and to whose inspiration we owe the pleasure of getting together at this historic place, the Klaffenbach Water Castle, to discuss problems of decisive importance for the unification of Europe and the world at large. By unification I do not refer to the incessantly discussed unification of Western Europe but rather to the unification of Europe as a whole, which to me seems to be an issue of even greater importance. But perhaps this aim has ultimately to be achieved via a previously established West European integration which, as we all know, has its own problems.

Coming from England to this conference, I am only too aware of the far-reaching nature of the sensitive issues surrounding European integration and the transition economies. The euro might help to unite Western Europe – let us hope that it will – but it could also in the end have disastrous consequences for some parts of euroland. Hopefully, this can be avoided.

However, we have gathered here to concentrate on Central and Eastern European economic problems and on the emergence of their money and capital markets in particular. The papers and discussants' comments have given us a much clearer idea of the tremendous complexities of the underlying difficulties our friends in those parts of Europe have been faced with since the breakdown of the Soviet Union. But we have also learned of their struggle to get their economies, and in particular their financial system, under control – some have been more successful than others.

Too often the transition countries are lumped together because they previously formed an entity under the leadership of the Soviet Union. In reality they could not be more different in the problems they had and are still having to face and in the success achieved in recent years. The magnitude of the Russian problems is immense and just cannot be compared with those of the more westernized countries of Eastern Europe, such as the Czech Republic, Hungary and Poland. East Germany again falls into quite a different category.[1,2] Here the Bundesbank system took over as central bank with the replacement of the East German Mark by the DM, while the big West German commercial banks simply extended their branch network throughout the new Länder in East Germany.[3]

But everywhere the shock caused by the change from a centrally planned to a market-based economy went much deeper than initially anticipated. In the monetary sector the previous main task was to direct money to meet enterprises' deficits; this required a large staff and branch network. The new aim was to influence economic behaviour by means of indirect instruments of monetary policy to control both interest rates and exchange rates, and to conduct the prudential supervision of the new commercial banks.

Suddenly the countries concerned had to acquaint themselves with methods of analysing economic data with the aim of acquiring knowledge concerning the behaviour of markets, firms and consumers. It would have been quite wrong to expect these new goals to change the process of decision-making overnight – even in those countries where the changes were immediately incorporated in the new constitutional laws.

But there was another shock, and that was the move from a monobank to a two-tier banking system. Under the old system there were really two monetary circuits: First, cash used mainly by individuals, and second the transfer between bank accounts used by enterprises. Thus, monetary policy was not just a matter of regulating the supply of money in circulation; there was also the credit-granting by each country's central bank to the public sector and enterprises, which often increased inflationary pressures. With the introduction of a competitive market system, an entirely new financial sector was required to regulate monetary matters. As Stephan (1999, p. 106) has pointed out, it was not enough to switch from a monobank to a two-tier banking system, but a dynamic capital market, too, with the necessary institutional set-up had to be created virtually from scratch. Most parts of the East European bloc suffered from a shortage of national savings. With private savings being largely absorbed by the State via budget deficits and other forms of public spending, respective central banks could scarcely be expected to provide for additional real resources by simply following a soft monetary policy.

The conditions for converting a centrally controlled economy into a market-based one obviously depends on a whole range of factors. We have to look at the size of the country concerned; we just cannot compare the problems faced by Russia with those of the smaller East European countries, especially as in Russia the old system has prevailed for a considerably longer time, in fact since the end of the World War II. Important, too, is the degree of true democracy achieved by the new regime. We also have to look at the sources of foreign exchange. Countries depending on foreign loans, whether private or granted by the IMF, the World Bank or other international financial institutions, are obviously in a weaker state than those where the source of foreign exchange is derived from external revenues – with the export of gas, oil and in some cases military equipment often playing a significant role.

Some of the transition countries are anxious to join the EU and even to become part of euroland. To realize these ambitions will require severe economic policies to get the economy into harmony with existing EU countries. EMU membership necessitates central bank independence and, if part of the single currency, the acceptance of the monetary policy conducted by the European Central Bank (ECB) for the whole of euroland. Some of the smaller transition countries are well on the way to achieving some of these goals and thanks to their liberalizing financial reforms have introduced financial policies and institutional structures not too far from those existing in euroland. This is encouraging and should be supported by their Western neighbours. Nevertheless, there are cases where a greater degree of harmonization with EU law and practice is still needed. But a basic question remains, namely the extent to which transition economies, however advanced, would really benefit from joining the euro with all the restrictions over monetary, exchange rate and fiscal policy this would involve. If their aspirations are more political – in other words a wish to become part of a likely European Federation – then acceptance of the strait jacket imposed by the Maastricht Treaty may be understandable.

It is sad to see the drastic setback in Russia with the virtual destruction of their financial sector in August 1998. As a result financial reforms and market-based financial transactions are increasingly viewed with considerable scepticism. The tendency there is rather retrograde with free markets being increasingly subjected to more discretionary administrative controls. Yet the financial position of at least 12 out of the 89 Russian regions remained quite favourable and some of them ignored the moratorium of the Federal Government and timely served their domestic and international debts after August 1998 (see the chapter by Vladislav Semenkov in this volume).

What has emerged from the papers and discussants' comments presented at the conference are numerous issues still to be investigated in greater depth – questions such as the degree of central bank independence, the issue of monetary versus inflation targets[4] and questions regarding the exchange rate system: should it be fixed or floating? Any financial reform must also be fully understood and supported by the general public. If accepted by both the government and parliament, the acceptance must be based on a clear understanding that central bank independence totally excludes any enforcement of subsidized credits to selected sectors of the economy. To ensure monetary stability the government must also develop non-monetary means of financing budget deficits and this will require smoothly operating money and capital markets which can only exist in a climate of political stability and a high degree of credibility of the central bank in its pursuit of optimal monetary targets. These prerequisites do not exist in Russia at present, and with few exceptions to a limited extent only in other Central and East European countries.

Nevertheless, it was encouraging to hear from some of the conference speakers of the success of reform policies in their respective country. The achievements of the Czech Republic, Hungary and Poland in particular are quite remarkable despite the problems they are still struggling with in creating effective money and capital markets. But these problems are at least in part not unrelated to the present volatility of international capital markets.

Indeed, if we look around us, we find that the transition countries are not the only ones facing difficulties. In the past 25 years, almost all countries throughout the world have experienced periods of severe financial turbulences, and sometimes with devastating effects on economic activity with world-wide repercussions.

At the same time, we have seen an increased liberalization of capital flows and financial systems generally. Financial markets, now playing a far greater role, turned increasingly into globalized international financial markets – no longer subject to effective national controls. These developments then led to increasing concern that the huge and largely uncontrolled international capital movements, of which only a minor part relates to the actual finance of foreign trade, would lead to a degree of financial volatility that could only prove harmful to the world economy.

An efficient control of international capital flows requires improved bank regulations and supervision. Only then will international capital inflows be prevented from producing a lending boom and dangerous risk-taking by banking institutions, as happened in the mid and late 1970s through the flow of OPEC surpluses to the London eurodollar market. Nothing else will ultimately prevent further severe episodes of financial instability. The now proposed establishment of a World Financial Authority (WFA) to complement the World Trade Organization (WTO), which also comprises the mandate to further high rates of employment and growth (see Eatwell and Taylor, 1998, Tietmeyer, 1999), and the subsequent Tietmeyer Plan for setting up a Financial Stability Forum, submitted to and accepted by the G-7 Finance Ministers and Central Bank Governors in February 1999, are important steps to develop policies to manage systemic financial risks.

However, some financial volatility must be accepted as an unavoidable feature of financial market operations, but special attention is required to detect in time when specific changes in asset prices occur which might raise the vulnerability of international financial markets to monetary instability.

We Europeans are now at a turning point. We owe it to our common cultural heritage to bring the whole of Europe together again in a hopefully peaceful world, but not necessarily on a federal basis. This will require sacrifices which will and should not be restricted to the Central and Eastern parts of Europe. Indeed, we Europeans – East and West – are and should all be involved in this process. I would go further by appealing to international financial institutions – the IMF, the World Bank and others – to be liberal in the provision of well supervised funds to Central and Eastern Europe. We have to ensure, of course, that these funds are neither mismanaged nor disappearing into the private pockets of some citizens in one way or another. But this is only ensured in a climate of political stability which should be the top priority of all transition countries.

A question mark remains in my view over the benefits for even the best-organized and successful of the central European countries to join

EMU. This issue is quite distinct from the obvious benefit of membership of the EU and the European single market.

Mr Chairman, a meeting and discussions in depth, like the ones you have so successfully organized, are of immeasurable benefit, not least because of the personal contacts they enable one to establish. I am sure of speaking in the name of all delegates to your conference in expressing our gratitude to the Technische Universität Chemnitz, its Economics Faculty and not least to Professor Jens Hölscher for an event which has brought us much further towards an understanding of a vital part of European developments close to the beginning of our new millennium. But our thanks are also due to the farsightedness of the Commerzbank in establishing the Stiftungslehrstuhl at the TU Chemnitz, and to the extent to which they – and not least the General Manager of the Commerzbank's Chemnitz Branch, Herr Ilbertz – have so generously personally as well as financially supported our conference.

Notes

* This chapter is an only slightly revised version of the pre-dinner speech given by Stephen F. Frowen on the occasion of the close of the conference these proceedings are based on [the editor].
1 For a wide-ranging study of the economic transition of East Germany, see, for example, Hölscher and Hochberg (1998). See also Frowen (1997) and, specially for the controversy over the conversion rate, Kloten (1998).
2 Karl-Heinz Paqué (1998, p. 15) has pointed out that the East German industrial base has now been reduced to a small, viable core of firms through privatization, but employing less than 14 per cent of the East German labour force. See also Claus Köhler (1997).
3 In a thorough study of the econnomic transition in Hungary and East Germany, Johannes Stephan (1999) uses East Germany as a case study for analysing the effect of the instant and complete systemic shift from a socialized planned economy to a competitive monetary system. This model is then applied to predict the performance of transition countries in general, but of Hungary in particular, under the changed economic system. The study clearly shows the advantages of the Hungarian gradualism and catch-up development over East Germany's premature integration. Of course, the latter was principally due to political considerations at the time of German unification.
4 On the issue of the feasibility and conditionality of inflation targeting in Central European countries for the EU accession, see Orlowski (1999).

References

Eatwell, J. and Taylor, L. (1998) *International Capital Markets and the Future of Economic Policy. A Report to the Ford Foundation*, IPPR Working Paper, London: Institute for Public Policy Research.

Frowen, S. F. (1997) The Dimensions of German Economic Unification – Keynote Address, in S. F. Frowen and J. Hölscher (eds), *The German Currency Union of 1990: A Critical Assessment*, London: Macmillan; New York: St Martin's Press, 1–12.

Hölscher, J. and Hochberg, A. (eds) (1998) *East Germany's Economic Development since Unification: Domestic and Global Aspects*, London: Macmillan; New York: St Martin's Press.

Kloten, N. (1998) German Unification: A Personal View, in S. F. Frowen and R. Pringle (eds), *Inside the Bundesbank*, London: Macmillan; New York: St Martin's Press, 110–19.

Köhler, C. (1997) The Privatisation of the East German Economy – The Role of the Treuhandanstalt, in S. F. Frowen and J. Hölscher (eds), *The German Currency Union of 1990: A Critical Assessment*, London: Macmillan; New York: St Martin's Press, 151–68.

Orlowski, L. T. (1999) *Feasibility and Conditionality of Inflation Targeting among Central European Candidates for the EU Accession*, Forschungsreihe of the Institut für Wirtschaftsforschung Halle (Saale), Germany, 2.

Paqué, K.-H. (1998) From Miracle to Crisis? The German Economy at the End of the Twentieth Century, in J. Hölscher and A. Hochberg (eds), *East Germany's Economic Development since Unification: Domestic and Global Aspects*, London: Macmillan; New York: St Martin's Press, 3–19.

Stephan, J. (1999) *Economic Transition in Hungary and East Germany: Gradualism and Shock Therapy in Catch-up Development*, London: Macmillan; New York: St Martin's Press.

Tietmeyer, H. (1999) International Cooperation and Coordination in the Area of Financial Market Supervision and Surveillance, Deutsch, Bundesbank, *Monthly, Report*, May, pp. 5–13.

16
Real Income Risk and Hedging in Transition Economies: A Note on Stephen F. Frowen

Harald L. Battermann and Udo Broll

1 Introduction

As mentioned by Stephen F. Frowen in his remarks on 'financial markets in transition countries', we concentrate on Central and Eastern European economic problems and on the emergence of financial markets. The economic conditions for converting a centrally organized economy into a market-oriented one obviously depend on a whole range of economic and institutional factors (see, for example, Bald and Nielsen, 1998; Hölscher, 1999; Sinel'nikow-Murilev and Trofimov, 1998). Nevertheless, economies in transition and re-emerging markets are attracting the attention of futures exchanges and international investors. This is illustrated by the futures contracts introduced recently by the Chicago Mercantile Exchange (CME), CME's newly established growth and emerging markets division, and the association of the Chicago Board of Trade with Argentinian, Polish, and Taiwanese authorities to establish futures exchanges in these countries.

The observed volatility in key macro variables, increased globalization and larger magnitude of exchanges of goods, services and financial assets make it necessary for international firms, especially in economies in transition, to hedge against the risk that may accompany international transactions (Halpern and Wyplosz, 1997; Lessard, 1995).

For instance, the risk represented by the volatility of spot foreign exchange rates is likely to lower international trade. However, a well established result shows that the introduction of a forward market is desirable to promote international trade (see, for example, Broll and Wahl, 1998).

Most of the discussions regarding hedging decisions of a risk averse international firm in the literature assume that the decision maker cares about nominal uncertain profits. Nominal profits are uncertain since the spot exchange rate of the next period is unknown. Exporting firms can protect themselves against exchange risk by using derivatives markets. If a currency forward market exists and if the forward market is unbiased then the optimal hedge ratio is one, in other words, a full hedge policy is optimal (see, for example, Lence, 1995; Kawai and Zilcha, 1986). However, this result depends on the assumption that the domestic price level is certain, i.e., real profits are uncertain due to uncertain nominal profits only. With regard to transition economies, our analysis differs from the traditional approach by considering that the domestic price level is not necessarily certain. Decision makers should not neglect real risks, since they are also consumers. Therefore, we distinguish between nominal and real income risks. Nominal income risk means that nominal profits are uncertain only, i.e., the domestic price level is certain. In case of real income risk the domestic price level is also uncertain. Does this distinction have an impact on the optimal hedge policy? It can be shown that the degree of relative risk aversion has an important impact on the optimal hedge ratio, i.e., the nominal and the real risk hedging approach differ systematically.

The plan of the chapter is as follows. In the next section we present the traditional full-hedge theorem first. Optimal hedging in a transition economy where the domestic price level is uncertain is discussed next. In the last section we summarize the main results.

2   Income risk and hedging

Consider a risk averse exporting firm in a transitionary economy. The firm exports a commodity X to the world market at time 1. Let the price of the commodity in the foreign country be Q and assume that it is fixed. At time 0 nominal income $\tilde{\Pi}$ in units of the domestic currency, say rouble, is uncertain due to an uncertain exchange rate $\tilde{e}$, where the tilde refers to uncertain variables. Denote by $e = g(s)$ the future exchange rate if the economy is in state $s = 1, 2$, so that $\tilde{e} = g(\tilde{s})$. The function g, and hence the distribution of the exchange rate, will not be determined endogenously, reflecting the partial equilibrium nature of our analysis.[1]

The firm can hedge risky income by selling or buying the quantity H on the forward market. The current forward price e_f relates to delivery at time 1. Then risky nominal income is given by

$\tilde{\Pi}(h) = \tilde{e}(1 - h)QX + hQXe_f$, where $h = H/QX$ denotes the hedge ratio. To make the analysis simple we assume that the forward market is in unbiased, i.e., the expected exchange rate equals the forward rate: $e_f = E(\tilde{e})$, where E is the expectations operator and the expectation is over the realization of states.

2.1   Nominal risk and hedging

Let us illustrate the optimal hedge ratio provided the decision maker is a risk averse expected utility maximizer[2] to whom income in real terms $\tilde{\Pi}_r = \tilde{\Pi}(h)/P$ matters, where P denotes the domestic price level. Throughout the chapter let us assume that preferences can be represented by a twice continuously differentiable utility function U.

As mentioned before, in this section we assume that the domestic price level P is certain and that the forward market is unbiased. In this case expected real income will not be affected by changes in the hedge ratio. Due to risk aversion the optimal hedge ratio is one. Loosely speaking, the decision maker chooses a hedge ratio such that 'marginal utility of roubles' ($dU/d\Pi$) is equalized in both states of nature.

2.2   Real risk and hedging

Now let us discuss the case when the domestic price level is also uncertain, i.e., we have to replace the domestic price level by $\tilde{P}$ where $P = f(s)$. The function f is exogenously given, so that $\tilde{P} = f(\tilde{s})$. Since the domestic price level is uncertain the firm can use the nominal hedging instrument (forward contracts) as an indirect hedging tool in order to hedge part of the price risk. Indirect hedging is possible if the exchange rate is correlated to the domestic price level $\tilde{P}$. In the following let us assume that the correlation is strongly positive[3] and that the forward market is unbiased. As before, the decision maker wants to equalize marginal utility in both states of nature.[4] However, marginal utility varies (in general) if the domestic price level changes. Hence optimal hedging depends on how marginal utility is related to the domestic price level. The relationship is positive (negative) if the degree of relative risk aversion is greater (less) than one.[5] Therefore, whether a hedge ratio greater or less than one is optimal depends on the decision maker's degree of relative risk aversion. For example, if the degree of relative risk aversion is greater than one then it is optimal to take a hedge ratio less than one. Due to the positive correlation between $\tilde{e}$ and $\tilde{P}$ a hedge ratio less than one stabilizes marginal utility between both states.

3 Concluding remarks

Risk management is the discipline of identifying risks in the business cycle, assessing their potential impact, and employing direct and indirect means for either reducing the exposure of underlying economic activities to these risks or shifting some of the exposures to others, if possible. Hedging risk by offsetting a spot market position with an opposite one in futures and forward contracts is important for firms in emerging markets and transition economies which are concerned with both the nominal and real risk of their operations. Since exchange rates and prices are volatile, and we also assume that increased globalization is likely to increase trade participation in transitionary countries, the demand for hedging in transition economies is likely to increase.

If governments of transition economies are willing and competent to create appropriate institutional arrangements for risk sharing, for example forward markets, the related empirical literature shows that hedging provides an effective risk reduction policy. According to the full-hedge theorem of the literature, it is optimal to fully hedge nominal income as long as the forward market is unbiased. However, our example demonstrates that it may not be optimal to choose a nominal full-hedge policy. The decision maker can use forward contracts as an indirect hedging instrument in order to reduce the risk of loss of purchasing power.

Notes

1 It should be noted that our findings do not depend on the two-state-approach. However, assuming that only two states are possible simplifies the analysis (see also Battermann and Broll, 1998).
2 A risk averse decision maker dislikes any mean-preserving spread in the sense of Rothschild and Stiglitz, 1970.
3 Loosely speaking, strong positive correlation means that a positive relationship between two random variables is preserved under monotone increasing transformations. A definition of strong correlation can be found in Battermann and Broll, 1997.
4 Due to our assumption that the forward market is unbiased, the optimal hedging rule reads (see, for example, Briys and Schlesinger, 1993; Broll and Eckwert, 1998):

$$U'(\Pi(h^*)/f(1))1/f(1) = U'(\Pi(h^*)/f(2))1/f(2).$$

Hence the decision maker chooses the optimal hedge ratio h^* in a way such that 'marginal utility of roubles' $(dU/d\Pi)$ is equalized in both states.
5 $(\partial/\partial P)(\partial/\partial\Pi)U = (1/P^2)(-U''(\Pi/P)\Pi/P - U'(\Pi/P)).$

References

Bald, J. and Nielsen, J. (1998), Developing Efficient Financial Institutions in Russia, *Communist Economies & Economic Transformation*, 10, 81–93.

Battermann, H. L. and Broll, U. (1997) *The Use of Derivatives Markets for Hedging Currency Risks*, University of München, Department of Economics, Working Paper, 97–18.

Battermann, H. L. and Broll, U. (1998) *Futures Markets and Hedging Real Profit Risk*, University of München, Department of Economics, Working Paper, 98–08.

Briys, E. and Schlesinger, H. (1993) Optimal Hedging when Preferences are State Dependent, *The Journal of Futures Markets*, 13, 441–51.

Broll, U. and Eckwert, B. (1998) Export and Hedging Decision with State-dependent Utility, *International Review of Economics and Finance*, 7, 247–53.

Broll, U. and Wahl, J. E. (1998) Missing Risk Sharing Markets and the Benefits of Cross-hedging in Developing Countries, *Journal of Development Economies*, 55, 43–56.

Halpern, L. and Wyplosz, C. (1997) Equilibrium Exchange Rates in Transition Economies, *IMF Staff Papers*, 44, 430–61.

Hölscher, J. (1999) Social Cohesion and Transition Dynamics, in I. Collier, H. Roggemann, O. Scholz and H. Tomann (eds), *Welfare States in Transition: East and West*, London: Macmillan Press, New York: St Martin's Press.

Kawai, M. and Zilcha, I. (1986) International Trade with Forward-futures Markets under Exchange Rate and Price Uncertainty, *Journal of International Economics*, 20, 83–98.

Lence, S. H. (1995) On the Optimal Hedge under Unbiased Futures Prices, *Economics Letters*, 47, 385–8.

Lessard, D. R. (1995) Financial Risk Management for Developing Countries: A Policy Overview, *Journal of Applied Corporate Finance*, 8, 4–18.

Rothschild, M. and Stiglitz, J. (1970) Increasing Risk: I. A Definition, *Journal of Economic Theory*, 2, 225–43.

Sinel'nikow-Murilev, S. and Trofimov, G. (1998) Fiscal Crisis and Macroeconomic Policy in Russia, *Communist Economies & Economic Transformation*, 10, 189–202.

Index

Note: 'n.' after a page reference indicates the number of a note on that page.